THE ULTIMATE SMALL BUSINESS GUIDEBOOK

THE UNUSUAL AND LOW-RISK SECRETS TO GENERATING PREDICTABLE REVENUE, SUCCESSFULLY LAUNCHING NEW PRODUCTS & SERVICES, AND DEVELOPING EFFECTIVE SYSTEMS FOR GROWTH AND PERSONAL FREEDOM

Ian M. Watts

The Small Business Dream Fulfillment Coach

SB Dream Coach
Grand River WorkPlace
19120 Grand River
Detroit, MI 48223

ISBN: 10: 1542848628

ISBN-13: 978-1542848626

Printed in the United States of America.

In an effort to support local communities, raise awareness and funds, a percentage of all book sales will be donated to non-profit organizations.

To learn more, visit: www.theusbg.com.

This book is available at quantity discounts for bulk purchases. For more information, please call 313-744-2003.

DEDICATION

To My God – I thank You for the privilege of being in Your service. I pray that this book pleases You as I fulfill my assigned mission to Build Businesses that Bless the World.

To My Wife – You are still "...my latest, my greatest inspiration." Words always fall short when expressing my love and deep appreciation for you. You are everything that I hoped for and even more than I dreamed. Your unfailing love and unwavering support allow me to keep pushing.

To My Kids – I hope that the small business work that daddy does and the impact of this book makes you proud and the sacrifice worth it. Daddy loves you!

To My Mom – I've heard that love is doing what's best for others though it may cost you a lot. Thank you for loving me with an unreasonable love and your subtle, yet unending encouragement.

To My Fellow Business Owners - I hope that my story encourages and my writing empowers you to build the Small Businesses of Your Dreams. I wrote this book to "Be What I Didn't See" as a Young Business Owner.

Table of contents

INTRODUCTION

Most businesses end in failure, broken dreams and in many cases, uncertain, stressful, and unfulfilled lives. Unfortunately, there are too many entrepreneurs starting businesses that will fail or never reach their full potential. A truly successful business is (1) one that is growing – consistently increasing in revenue and profitability, (2) that can function without the owner, (3) and that provides the passive income so that you, the owner, can live the life of your dreams. Unfortunately, very few businesses meet these criteria. And, it normally isn't for lack of effort. There are so many entrepreneurs who work themselves into poor health, failed marriages, estranged relationships with kids and sometimes multiple bankruptcies, only to find that they are still missing the mark. If hard work alone isn't going to allow you to realize the small business success that you are working toward, there must be more to it. There are still gaps that need to be filled in. Unfortunately, discovering exactly what those gaps are is a monumental challenge. If it weren't such a challenge, there probably wouldn't be a need for this book and many more entrepreneurs would reach the goals that they dream of.

The Ultimate Small Business Guidebook fills in the gaps and reveals the unusual and low-risk secrets to generating predictable revenue, successfully launching new products and services, and developing effective systems for growth and personal freedom. Unfortunately, there is a great deal of noise surrounding the general topic of small business success. It's noisy because there are so many people who have joined the conversation, written books, and offered training to provide "THE SOLUTION." Just do a quick Google search on "small business success" or do a quick search on Amazon. The number of results that you will get is astounding. As a matter of fact, while writing I did a Google search and came up with 129,000,000 search results. Results like that are completely overwhelming. This is especially the case when the stakes are so high for you, as a business owner. At best, most people select a few books that help them inch toward success. And, in some cases, great setbacks are caused by listening to the wrong advice. I am all too familiar with some of these setbacks.

I am fortunate to have achieved my dream of becoming a millionaire by the age of 26, just less than four years ahead of my personal goal. But I didn't do so without a lot of struggle. I know what it is to work so hard that you make yourself sick. I know what it's like to be so engulfed in business that relationships are damaged. While I do believe in sacrifice, I don't believe that your most precious relationships should be sacrificed at the altar of success. And, I also know what it's like to fail and have to file for bankruptcy. So, in many ways, this book is what I would have written to my younger self so that I could avoid the pitfalls of growing a successful business and so that I could grow it much faster.

Most of us are familiar with Vilfredo Pareto's 80/20 Principle. If only 20% of what we do in our businesses accounts for 80% of the results, we would all do well to identify and prioritize the most important 20% of activities that will allow us to build the businesses of our dreams. I wrote this book so that you don't have to continue to work yourself into the ground without getting the results that you are looking for. I wrote this book to teach you the 20%. I wrote this book to "be what I didn't see" as a young business owner. My goal is to help you accelerate your path to success while avoiding the pitfalls that so many fall prey to.

The Ultimate Small Business Guidebook will cut through all of the noise and help you discover:

- The 2 Unusual Secrets that Will Immediately Transform Your Business
- How to Develop Predictable and Sustainable Revenue
- How to Avoid the Stress, Wasted Time & Money of Growing Your Small Business
- How to Develop Business Systems that Allow You to Scale Your Business and Give You Personal Freedom
- How to Develop a Model to Quickly and Inexpensively Test Any New Business, Product or Service Idea to Ensure that it is Irresistible to Your Market
- The 7 Secrets of the World's Most Successful Entrepreneurs
- So Much More Good Stuff...

Because I want you to hurry and get going, I won't bore you with too many testimonials. But I will share just one so that you can truly embrace what *The Ultimate Small Business Guidebook* will do for you. "Ian is one of the most brilliant entrepreneurs and small business coaches that I know. Using the principles in this book, he developed an innovative system that allowed me to rapidly grow my company from 6 clinics to 61 clinics nationwide, hiring over 300 people in less than 2 years. This was done with a third of the usual staffing." - Rich Morgan, President, LightRx Face and Body; he built and sold the largest laser aesthetics company in the world, with over 230 clinics and 1800 employees.

When writing this book, I asked myself if there was only one, concise, practical, step-by-step book in the world that I could read on the topic of small business success, would *The Ultimate Small Business Guidebook* pass the test? I recognize that I am biased. But, after reading more than 200 other business books, with a clear conscience and sober mind, I'm proud to say that this work would definitely be my small business bible.

Right here in the introduction, allow me to offer just one nugget. As you begin this book, you will quickly learn two secrets that will literally transform the way that you do business. But, before you get there, allow me to share one more secret. Honestly, this secret is so powerful that I wrestled with myself over where I should place it. But, here goes. The transformation that you are seeking will only happen when you take MASSIVE ACTION. Here is the reality: Information alone doesn't cause transformation. Application is what brings about change. And, this application must be done in an extreme or massive way. So, resist the temptation to delay. Don't wait! Say yes to yourself and yes to your small business dream. Immediately crack the book open to Chapter 1 so that you can then learn the unusual and low-risk secrets to generating predictable revenue, successfully launching new products and services, and developing effective systems for growth and personal freedom in your business.

Let's get it!

Ian

The Small Business Dream Fulfillment Coach

CHAPTER 1
'06 WAS A GOOD YEAR: WHY

"START WITH WHY." —SIMON SINEK

I can still remember 2006 as if it was yesterday. It really felt like a movie was playing and my wife and I were the unwitting stars. I'm sitting in a dark hospital room and had been there for several days. My wife, the patient, whom I had been staring at for the past two hours, was peacefully asleep. While she slept, I was consumed with the reality that I had lost my business, had lost several loved ones, and now I faced the real possibility of losing not only my unborn daughter and first child, but my wife as well. It was the last quarter in 2006. And it was easily the most difficult time that I have ever experienced.

Let's take a journey back in time. I had dreams of being a millionaire. Not only that, it was my goal to achieve that dream by the time I was 30. And I did it! I achieved my dream. I had done it by the age of 26, just under four years ahead of my goal. I knew what it was to grind from sunup to sundown. I knew what it was to be so consumed with success and achieving my goal that I could be having a conversation with you but be in a completely different place, calculating numbers, considering which deals I had going, what business I wished I could get back to. The business I was in was real estate. And, I had gained the nickname of Mr. Trump. (Allow me to say that having the Trump name was a bit more endearing in many more circles than it is now.)

Let's go back a bit more. In many ways, the early story of my life is familiar to many who grow up in urban areas across the United States. I grew up on the east side of Detroit and was on welfare. My brother, Branden, who is four years my senior, and I were raised by a single mother. This isn't because my father split and we didn't know where he was. Actually, he wasn't around because he was away at "school," as my mom described it. It turns out that school happened to be at Jackson State Penitentiary. My mom is going to read this. So, in fairness to her, let me say that my father was in school and did actually complete his undergraduate degree with honors. It just happened to be in a place where he couldn't freely come and go!

Even though I grew up poor, my early childhood years were really happy. I had to get a little bit older to learn the realities of living on less than $580 per month. Allow me to say that, even though we didn't have much, we were clean, we ate (even though it was often not what we wanted), our clothes were ironed, and my mom instilled great character and pride. Yet I can also say that I know what it is to use wet newspaper as toilet tissue, to not have utilities, and to be constantly disappointed with broken promises about new clothes, shoes, and toys. Having said this, I can't begin to thank my mom enough for the sacrifices that she made for my brother and me. I can remember her catching the bus to school with my brother and me, then catching the bus herself to Wayne State University, where she would eventually graduate. It took her seven years to get her undergraduate degree, but she did it. And she has now been a teacher in Detroit Public Schools for over 20 years. My mom is a pillar of strength. For her, I am truly grateful.

Watching my mom's strength and helped by her encouragement, I was convinced that there wasn't much that I couldn't do. This worked out really well for me because, the more I saw my mom struggle, the more impassioned I became about helping her in any way I could. Honestly, I took this a bit too far. I became convinced that the answer to all problems, or at least all our struggles, was money. And I was determined to get it.

In my early teens, I resolved that I was going to be a small business success, no matter what it took. Consequently, I absolutely hated school. The delay in payoff was too great. It felt like a complete waste of time. I couldn't identify much with the other kids. I had serious stuff on my mind, not the "normal" concerns of any of the kids around me, as far as I could tell. There were a few bright spots in school, though. Every now and then I was able to laugh. I have always been a silly guy. Yet there were no jokes funny enough to mask the pain and passion so deep that it consumed me. Most of the time when I was in school, I wrestled with the delayed satisfaction that school offered. Getting good grades, going to college, and getting a good job didn't do anything for the immediacy of needs or desires that I had for my family and me.

In came Carlton Sheets. While I had done several things to make money—a paper route (when I was too young), reselling candy, and cutting hair, where I made really good money—the business that catapulted me to early success was in real estate. He doesn't come on anymore but, when

I was about 16 years old, I watched a late night infomercial about Carlton Sheets and his No Money Down Real Estate Investment System. You know the commercial: Carlton is on the balcony of his mansion. He is sitting with his legs crossed in slacks with creases sharper than razors and a crisp button up as he interviews one of his students about how his real estate investment system can make you rich.

I got it. Investing in real estate would be my ticket to millions. I got hold of the system and I was all in. When I started with Carlton Sheets' system, I was 16 years old and I studied it for almost two years straight. And, using his system, I was able to purchase my first house, with no money down (of my own) at the age of 19. Actually, I'll be honest and say that my first deal actually wasn't that good. I paid too much, made too little, and didn't have any financial reserve in case things went south (and they did). But my second deal, not much later, was a beauty. I was able to purchase a home, get over $19,000 at closing and still have good cash flow and equity left in the home. I was in business now. I just had to do the same thing a lot of times and I would build net worth, passive income, and liquidity that would set me up for life.

I did it. I went from one success to the next. In fact, I did the same type of deals, over and over again. And, before I knew it, I had actually achieved my goal and become a millionaire. My wife and I had "his and hers" Lexuses, the deals were moving, the cash was coming in, and we were able to purchase our dream house. Actually, this house we beyond our dreams. As it turned out, it was a builder's dream house, literally. We found a house in a subdivision where the builder had built a home for himself and his family after he had built all of the other homes in the sub and it was amazing. Picture this: The front yard was a part of the golf course for our country club community (I forget which hole). The backyard was a small lake. The house had a total of almost 10,000 square feet of living space. There were five bedrooms, six bathrooms, four-car heated garage on the upper level and an additional two-car garage on the lower level. Not only all of that, but this house had features like remote fireplaces, doggy showers, and a retractable chandelier. Seriously, it was an amazing house. And, because the builder ended up having some family challenges, this amazing house was now ours. Imagine that! All of this house for just my beautiful, pregnant wife and me. We felt like we were on top of the world.

As you probably guessed, as is common in the lives of entrepreneurs, major problems eventually arose. During this time, I got really good at doing deals and my deals had become larger and more plentiful. However, doing deals was the NOT the same thing as building a sustainable business that could operate without me. (I will discuss this further in Chapter 10.) Along the way, I came to realize that I was really looking for financial freedom. I wanted to build a life in which my passive income, meaning money that I didn't need to actively work for on a monthly basis, exceeded my monthly needs and desires. Actually, I had some notion of this when I began in real estate. However, the lump sums of cash became hypnotic and I went from one deal to the next without true regard for building passive income. I finally came to understand that this needed to change, so my wife and I set out to build a business that would truly give us the passive income that we were looking for. The problem arose because it was too little, too late. The misstep of becoming deal junkies proved to be disastrous. When we decided to put things into high gear to build a business properly, we found ourselves with the recession kicking into high gear as well. And there was trouble.

I failed. I failed miserably. I failed and lost everything. We lost millions in assets, pretty much all of our assets. We lost that dream house that I described. We went from living in a house that was almost 10,000 square feet in a golf community to living in a single room in my father-in-law's house. We lost our cars. I lost several hundred thousand dollars of investors' cash. In short, while the economic sky was falling in 2006, it made sure to stop by and visit us. We lost everything. Well, almost. Allow me to pause right here and be very clear about the fact that I am NOT blaming the recession for my business failure. My business failed because of a bad business model and because it was too heavily dependent upon financing. Now that I have covered that, here is what happened. My wife and I purchased two beautiful homes in an area called Palmer Park in Detroit. We were going to turn them into adult foster care homes. Actually, we were going to operate one and build the other out to partner with an owner-operator. My mother-in-law is a social worker and my brother is a nurse, so, we were pretty excited about this opportunity not just for us, but for our family as well. Unfortunately, this opportunity never materialized.

In the last quarter of 2006, I traveled on a mission trip with my church, Evangel Ministries, to Uganda. And, I was riding pretty high. I had gone from one success to the next, I was young and I was now finally getting my business where I wanted it to be. When I left, I was in the middle of multiple deals that I was refinancing. I was expecting to come back to over $400,000. Well, it didn't happen. As I communicated with my wife while in Africa, I learned that our deals were running into complications. For us, refinancing was nothing out of the ordinary, so learning of unexpected complications that came out of the blue for not just a few but all of our deals was distressing, to say the least. Eventually, for one reason or another, all of our deals fell apart and this was very damaging because we had sunk our cash into the new adult foster care home that we were scheduled to open in less than 60 days.

Back to the hospital room in 2006: We not only lost our business, but we also lost several close loved ones. And now, I'm in a hospital room praying that I don't lose my wife and unborn child. My wife was having a difficult pregnancy. My daughter, Mina, was trying to come too soon and my wife had some pretty serious blood issues. Sitting in that cold, dark hospital room, reflecting upon everything that happened, is a hard experience to express even now. But what I can share is that this experience gave me clarity of thought and purpose and was one of the major driving forces behind this book and my passion to serve entrepreneurs. Through this experience, I discovered my "WHY."

I realized that there are many things in life that I have absolutely no control over. I couldn't control the deaths of my loved ones. I had no control over what would happen to my wife and daughter. But I did have control over my business. And, had I been better equipped to build a business the right way, that would have made my experience in 2006 and the years immediately following a bit less traumatic. However, it's also because of my experience that I can write this book now. That experience reminded me of my commitment to "be what I didn't see" as a young business owner looking for mentorship that I didn't receive. My experience keeps me ever mindful of the underdog. My experience reinforced my personal mission to build businesses that bless the world. Not only can I help entrepreneurs avoid the spectacular business failure that I had experienced, but I can guide them to impact their families, communities, and the world with their businesses.

My wife and I now jokingly say that '06 was a good year. Yes, thankfully, my wife and my daughter, Mina, made it through that trial with good health and are doing well, along with my two other kids, Pierson and Ethan. And, while 2006 was an extremely difficult year, it was indeed good for a number of reasons, not the least of which was me discovering my personal mission. In short, that experience helped me to discover, my "WHY," my deep internal passion that informs and drives everything that I do. Allow me to close this chapter by encouraging you to do some introspection so that you, too, can discover your WHY. Without it, I can assure you that you won't make it. There is a reason why such a small percentage of people build highly successful businesses. And, it is NOT primarily a skill issue. Rather, it is an issue of will. If you have a strong enough will, you will have the resolve to learn, persevere, and develop the skills needed to succeed. You won't just read this book, but you will apply what you read, despite how you may feel at any given moment. Discovering your WHY will give you the internal driving force, the fuel, the WILL that allows you to keep pushing when all you want to do is quit. And, I can assure you, there will be times when you will be tempted to throw in the towel. It is even a possibility that you will experience your own version of 2006. But success is found on the other side of failure and after long periods of persistence through struggle.

Coaching Assignment: In one clear statement, write down what your "WHY" is.

Visit www.theusbg.com to download a FREE tool on discovering your WHY.

CHAPTER 2

SHUSH: TWO SECRETS THAT WILL CHANGE EVERYTHING

" IT AIN'T WHAT YOU DON'T KNOW THAT GETS YOU INTO TROUBLE. IT'S WHAT YOU KNOW FOR SURE THAT JUST AIN'T SO."—Mark Twain

Quickly, tell me what the picture below says:

████████████████████████████████

I f your answer to the question above is, "JUMPING TO CONCLUSIONS," you would be absolutely incorrect. Sorry, I couldn't resist. While the answer appears to be "JUMPING TO CONCLUSIONS," it actually says, "JUMRJNC TQ GQNGIUSIONS."

I regularly conduct free small business boot camps across the country. I do this because I want to make sure that I can provide the training that early-stage and established business owners need to build the businesses of their dreams. And, at the beginning of each boot camp, I do this quick exercise. Without fail, everyone answers the same. This is because we are wired to make sense of things based on our experiences. And, because of that, we still find it hard to let go of our beliefs, even when things are outdated or just plain wrong. Unfortunately, that leaves a great deal of room for mistakes in all areas and it stunts our ability to learn and grow. So, in an effort to combat this phenomenon of human nature, I included the example above. In this book, beginning in this very chapter, you are going to be exposed to things that will probably be very new to you. Some things will even be contrary to what you have learned throughout the years and have come to accept. But do me—and yourself—a favor. When you read something that seems to contradict some philosophies or practices that you have come to accept, remember the illustration above. Remember just how sure you were of the answer only to discover that what you thought was actually incorrect. This will allow you to go much further much faster as we progress together through this book.

Before my small business boot camps begin, I always spend time interacting with as many of the attendees as I can. And the one question that I ask every one of them is, "What business are you in?" And, undoubtedly, the answers that I receive are all wrong. The right answer to this question will absolutely change the entire trajectory of your small business. If you can embrace what I am about to share and act accordingly, your business and your life will NEVER be the same. Are you ready for it? Well, here it is -

SECRET #1: YOU ARE IN THE MARKETING BUSINESS

Remember, we made an agreement for you to be open-minded at the beginning of this chapter. At this point, I can probably guess what is going through your mind. You are thinking that you are not in the marketing industry. You are thinking that you run a landscaping company, a web design business, a dental office (fill in the blank). You are thinking that what you do, the service or product that you sell, is the business that you are in. But it is not. The product or service that you provide is the actual deliverable, or what Michael Gerber of E-myth Worldwide calls technical work. And, although technical work is important, you can't build a business that allows you the freedom of time and passive income to live the life that you dream of being the master of technical work. You actually have to build a different skill set so you can become a master of marketing.

If you want to build a successful small business, it has to be profitable. To generate profit, you have to have revenue that exceeds expenses. To generate revenue, you need to make sales. In order to make sales, you need consistent leads. And, finally, to generate consistent leads, you have to become an expert in marketing. For the sake of simplicity, I am going to reduce the definition of marketing to "positioning your business and your product or service to generate leads and create sales opportunities." After all, we live in a market-driven economy. The hope that all entrepreneurs should have when going into business is that they will produce and present a good or a service to a market that finds it valuable.

Have you ever seen the movie, "Field of Dreams?" This movie stars Kevin Costner, who is a corn farmer. In the movie, he begins to hear voices, which he interprets as a command to build a baseball diamond in his fields. The one line that I would like to draw your attention to is this: "If you build it, they will come." And come they did. After Kevin Costner's character built the baseball diamond, the

1919 White Sox team came. It was a pretty cool movie and I recommend that you watch it if you have the time. Unfortunately, too many people build their businesses based on the "...if you build it, they will come" model. Too many people think that customers, clients, and patients will simply flock to their businesses because they decided to open. I have a bit of a news flash: If you build it, they will NOT come. The line in the movie made for great cinema but is a horrible business practice. And this very business philosophy is driving businesses and families into the ground. I won't bore you with the stats because you can easily Google them. But most businesses fail because the owners thought that being a good technician and doing the technical work in the business was the same as being a good entrepreneur, doing work on the business.

One of the most effective ways to work on your business and not simply in it is by realizing that your job is to get really good at understanding, creating, and sharing with potential customers, clients or patients, how you can solve their pain and/or help them with their desires. And this is what good marketing does. I have another major news flash. Outside of close family and friends, no one cares that you have started a business. People only care about you starting a business to the extent that it benefits them. This is much more than just opening the doors, virtual or brick-and-mortar, to your business. This is truly the function of marketing. So, again, you are in the marketing business and your job is to get really good at this, as marketing is what brings the money in. Now that we have firmly established the fact that you are in the marketing business, we can move on to the next secret.

SECRET #2: YOU ARE IN THE SYSTEM BUILDING BUSINESS.

If you are reading this book, I am sure that you have an interest in building a business that will allow you to achieve financial freedom. The only thing that will allow you to build a business with the passive income (income that you are not actively working for) and freedom of time that you are looking for is a system. So, not only are you in the marketing business, but you are also in the system building business. If marketing is where the money is, building systems is where the freedom is. A system is a written and chronological set of instructions for all of the key areas in your business. All too often, people who are trying to build a business do so with a very limited view of what it takes to be a success. This is especially so in my own experience. I thought that learning how to do deals, which I was really good at, was the same as building a successful business. Doing deals is exactly the skill that I learned. The problem with this is that doing deals will never get you to the place where you want to be. Sure, you can make a lot of money doing deals. But, this is not the same as building a business that works without you so that it will continue to generate the income that you desire.

Too often when entrepreneurs begin to discuss systems, there is a haze of intimidation surrounding this subject. That's because it is misunderstood and made out to be more difficult than it actually is. Eventually, your systems will become more and more robust. And, you will use technology to automate as many functions as possible. But this happens gradually. Where you begin is not where you will end. I do indeed believe in beginning with the end in mind. Yet, everyone has to start somewhere. And, when starting to develop effective systems, I believe in taking a minimalist approach, doing just enough so that your business can function and expanding when necessary.

For most business owners, possibly including you, there is already a framework for how things are done. The problem is, it isn't written, it often changes, and it isn't the most efficient way of doing things. When thinking about your business, you have to ask yourself: "If I couldn't work in my business at all, what systems do I need to have in place and what people need to oversee these systems for my business to thrive?" Another way of viewing the power of systems is to think about your business as if it were an actual product on a shelf. Consider what this means for a moment. When you buy a product from a store, you expect the product to work the way it's supposed to work. So it is with your business. You have to create a business that actually works. One of the things that I love in the book *E-Myth* is when its author, Michael Gerber, says that you should create your business as if you are going to franchise it 5,000 times, even if you have no intention of building a franchise. The idea is that every area of your business functions so well that you could replicate the model thousands of times if you wanted to. Believe it or not, building systems is a far easier task than most people think.

Since you have now learned that you are in the marketing and system building business, it stands to reason that I will spend a significant amount of time walking you through how to market and build systems. No matter what your experience has been thus far, no matter what your unique strengths and weaknesses are, you will be able to walk away from this book with the tools and confidence needed to become proficient at both. Not only this, there are some additional, fundamental truths and skills that you will be exposed to that will also be transformative. I truly created this book with the idea that it would be a concise, yet power-packed reference guide for you. I didn't want it to be filled with a lot of motivation, although being motivated is important. I wrote this book to be the meat and potatoes that you need to take action. I am interested in you using this book as a primary tool for application, one that you could reference over and over again as you develop the business of your dreams. So, strap up and get ready for takeoff because we are about to embark upon a fast and furious journey, beginning with the next chapter, as we take a deep dive into the world of marketing.

Coaching Assignment: Re-read this chapter before moving on to the next chapter.

Visit www.theusbg.com to download free resources for chapter coaching assignments.

CHAPTER 3
SWOOSH:
TWO TYPES OF MARKETING

"JUST DO IT"—NIKE

I t is important to note that some of the most successful entrepreneurs are standing on the backs of other successful entrepreneurs. Success leaves clues. And we would do well to emulate success. The challenge that we run into is that we often model the wrong things. Keep this in mind, as we will come back to this point in this chapter shortly.

There may be people who will argue with this. But, for the purpose of simplicity, there are primarily two major types of marketing. The first type of marketing is called branding. If I were to ask whose company slogan "Just Do It" is, almost everyone in the modern world would reply that the company is Nike. If I told you to picture a red sign with two large golden arches, you, along with the rest of the world, can quickly tell me it is McDonald's. This is because McDonald's is one of the most recognizable brands in the world, if not the single most. There is a reason that you could quickly, without thinking, tell me exactly which companies I made mention of above with only a slogan or a picture. This is due to the power of branding. In short, branding works. And, because I mentioned that success leaves clues and that we should model success, we should focus on and invest our money into branding our businesses, right? Well, unfortunately, this thinking would be wrong. Yet, this is what so many of us have been taught and come to accept.

Well, if you shouldn't invest your money and time into branding your business in the hearts and minds of the market, following the clues from the most successful companies in the world, what should you do? I did mention that success leaves clues. And this is something that we will address more fully in the last chapter of this book. But, for now, allow me to simply state that you have to follow the right successes and the right clues. The reason that global brands are as recognizable as they are is because they have spent hundreds upon hundreds of millions of dollars on branding campaigns to become so. Recently, I read a stat that is a few years old now that said that one out of every six dollars in restaurant marketing is spent by McDonald's. Investing money into building a brand is not only costly but it is also extremely time-consuming. And major companies invest into branding for different reasons that you are investing into your marketing efforts. It is dangerous for you to model the activities of a business that has goals that are significantly different than yours. Major brands may invest in branding to increase shareholder value (if they're publicly traded) or to prepare for a major merger or acquisition. Your goal, however, is to do your best to figure out how you can get customers, clients, or patients in the door now. Your goal is to ensure that you can make payroll. As an entrepreneur, the very first goal of any business is to survive long enough to break even financially, where your revenue at least equals your expenses. Do a quick exercise: Stop for just a moment and hold your breath for as long as you can before reading further. If you actually did my little exercise, imagine what would have happened if right at the point where you had to take a breath, you discovered that you had to wait another few minutes. Well, you can quickly see how this is a problem and that maybe you would not have been able to survive, right? So it is with business and branding. Having cash flow is like oxygen to your business. And, even though there are long-term benefits to branding, it doesn't solve your immediate need for cash. Without marketing that produces immediate results, your business will die. Am I saying that you shouldn't build a brand? Absolutely not! But, what I am saying and what I am about to reveal to you is another type of marketing that all entrepreneurs should maximize, with branding being a byproduct. The second type of marketing and the type of marketing that you should focus on is direct response marketing.

Direct response marketing is designed to evoke an immediate response and compel prospects to take some specific action, such as opting into an email list, picking up the phone and calling for more information, placing an order, or being directed to a web page. The distinct difference between branding and direct response marketing is that the latter prompts you to take action now. Consider this: You are driving on the freeway and you see a swoosh sign from Nike that says, "Just Do It." That sign doesn't cause you to take immediate action. While it might be encouraging, while it is highly recognizable, we don't have the luxury of paying for such a sign as early-stage entrepreneurs. If you embrace the fact that you are in the marketing business and become really good at direct response marketing, it doesn't matter what business you decide to start or grow, you will do well. **The single greatest key to generating predictable revenue in your business is your ability to capture, cultivate, and convert cold traffic into sales.** And the best way to do this is by direct response marketing. In the next chapter, we will cover the ground rules of direct response marketing.

Coaching Assignment: Determine the return on investment of your marketing efforts for the last 30 days.

Visit www.theusbg.com to download a free return-on-investment tool.

CHAPTER 4
RULES OF THE GAME: DIRECT RESPONSE

"YOU HAVE TO LEARN THE RULES OF THE GAME. AND THEN YOU HAVE TO PLAY BETTER THAN ANYONE ELSE."—ALBERT EINSTEIN

Getting good at direct response marketing means you have to embrace a set of rules that will be contrary to much of what you have probably come to accept. Because I know that, throughout this entire book and especially on this subject, I am still slaying some giants in your thinking, allow me to further persuade you to throw out bad ideas that you have about branding and other poor marketing practices by first telling you some of the major benefits of direct response marketing.

Benefit #1: Direct response marketing will always provide measurable results. To an entrepreneur, cash is precious and you need to be able to account for how every single dollar is used. Whenever you invest money in marketing, you need to consider that your marketing letters or messages are salaried sales agents. Seriously consider this for a moment: If you had salaried sales agents responsible for selling your products or services, you would track very closely how much they sold on a regular basis. This is because you don't have the luxury of them telling you every single month that, "they didn't sell anything, but they did help to get our company name "out there." No, on the contrary. If they don't sell and provide measurable results, they wouldn't be able to remain on your staff. So it is with your marketing dollars. You need to be able to very clearly track the results that each marketing campaign yields, whether it uses direct mail, television, radio, online, or some other medium.

Benefit #2: Direct response marketing can provide up to ten times the return on investment as non-direct response marketing. Imagine this: You send out direct mail to prospective clients' homes or businesses. If you know anything about direct mail, you know that a 1% to 3% response rate—meaning 1% to 3% of the people take the action that your marketing piece called for them to take—you are doing extremely well by traditional standards. Now imagine that you are able to go all the way up to a 10% response rate. That means that 1 out of every 10 people respond to your marketing message. Those results seem too good to be true, right? Well, I can tell you from personal experience that I was able to do just that. And, while response rates that high are not common, direct response marketing will drastically increase your return on investment if you follow the ground rules.

Benefit #3: Direct response marketing allows you to attract your ideal customers, clients, and patients. How hard would it be for you to build a profitable and thriving business while absolutely hating the customers, clients, or patients that you are working with? It sounds crazy, right? But many people try to do it. This is because they don't know how to market properly and have to take what they can get when building their businesses. But it doesn't have to be, and shouldn't be, that way. As a matter of fact, your business is YOUR business and you should design it in a way that you are excited about. Marketing properly will help you to do this.

Benefit #4: Direct response marketing helps you to avoid price suppression. Too often entrepreneurs generate business by trying to undercut the prices of their competitors. And, in nine of ten cases, this is a horrible strategy. If your price is too low, more than likely you will have poor profit margins and poor profit margins won't allow you to grow your company. More on this in Chapter 7. The reason that entrepreneurs do this is because that is their best marketing effort. Becoming a good direct response marketer will allow you to introduce your product or service in a unique way that allows your customers, clients, or patients to be drawn to you, as opposed to their feeling that they are being pushed to do something or pursued as if they are in a shopping mall with a salesperson who won't leave them alone. One of the best ways to avoid devaluing your product or service is for the customer, client, or patient to feel like they are chasing you down instead of the other way around.

Benefit #5: Direct response marketing allows you to win even in a crowded market. At this point, I would like to shatter another common myth. Most of us have been taught that you shouldn't start a business unless it is something completely new and highly innovative. And, yes, introducing something new and innovative has its merit. However, in many cases, it is better to introduce something that the market has already shown that it wants. The trick is to introduce something highly unique about the business or what is called a unique selling proposition so that you stand out in the crowd. Sometimes, something completely new doesn't succeed because the market does not want it. So, allow me to give you permission (after finishing this book) to take a look at a few of the old business ideas that you abandoned because traditional wisdom told you to. By understanding how to position yourself and your business properly as a direct response marketer, you may decide that you have given up on a passion of yours and maybe you shouldn't have.

Benefit #6: Direct response marketing focuses on lead generation. Only a small percentage of the market is ready to buy anything right now. I have heard some estimates as low as 2%-6%. And it doesn't matter what industry you are in or what you are selling. So, one of the main benefits of direct response marketing is that it allows you to capture the information needed so you extend the reach of your marketing dollars. If such a small percentage of the population is ready to buy now and you have major brands spending billions of dollars per year to compete, you are not going to outspend them. You have to outthink and out-niche them, with a focus on presenting what you can uniquely offer to them as you continue to follow up so that, when they are ready to purchase, you will be the natural choice.

Benefit #7: Direct response marketing is systematized. Remember, you are not only in the marketing business; you are also in the system building business. If you are going to create a thriving business, your marketing efforts can't be sporadic. Direct response marketing forces you to develop the good discipline of doing things in a step-by-step process so that you can track and yield predictable results. When you have tested and become clear about the results that your marketing investment and systems should produce, the only thing that will keep you from growing your business will be how much can you spend on marketing and how quickly can you build the systems and capacity of your organization to service the business that you will bring in.

Hopefully, the seven benefits listed above have convinced you of the value of direct response marketing. Now, we can move on to the rules of direct response marketing, several of which will fly in the face of what you have learned and may or may not be doing now. So there are rules that you need to follow, habits that you will need to form, and some that you will probably need to break if you are going to build the business of your dreams.

7 Direct Response Marketing Rules:

Direct Response Marketing Rule #1: You will always have a specific, very well-defined target audience in mind. When you try to market to everyone, you market to no one. Broad, generic, catch-all messages will be the death of your marketing.

Direct Response Marketing Rule #2: There will always be strong copy/content. The content that is written (heard or seen) is truly salesmanship in print (audio or video) and should be treated as such. Good copy is what allows the sales conversion process to be simple. Thus, it eliminates the need to have the industry's top salespeople, which helps keep your business model scalable.

Direct Response Marketing Rule #3: There will always be an offer or offers. Unlike branding, an offer should always be presented whenever you deliver a marketing piece. Between marketing messages and the simple busyness of life, we are all getting more and more distracted by the minute, so having someone's attention is a precious gift. Because you don't know when or if you will ever get that person's attention again, you need to present them with an opportunity to do business with you. As a matter of fact, you do people a disservice when you open them up to the possibilities of what your company can provide without giving them an opportunity to say yes. They may end up saying yes to a competitor who does present an offer, even if the product or service offered is not half as good as yours. Both you and your prospective customer, client, or patient lose.

Direct Response Marketing Rule #4: There will always be clear instructions. You should always be leading your prospects down the path by providing steps for them to follow, and these next steps need to be explained very clearly. Confused buyers do not buy. This is something that most marketers struggle with. Even if the content of a marketing message is strong, it is often ruined by confusing instructions, often because they offer too many ways to take the next step in the relationship or process. Although it is done with the mindset of making things convenient, it often results in no action being taken.

Direct Response Marketing Rule #5: There will always be a reason to respond *now*. We have to help our prospects to do what is in their own best interest. It is amazing how sales-averse we all are. Even when we need a product or service, want it, and can afford it, there is still an emotional reaction that often makes it hard to say yes, even when we should. Giving people reasons to respond immediately helps them clear this hurdle.

Direct Response Marketing Rule #6: There will always be tracking and clear metrics. You need to run your marketing and entire business by the numbers. I mentioned earlier that you should treat your marketing dollars as salaried sales agents. This means that you have to demand accountability for every dollar that is invested in marketing so that you are very clear about what is and is not effective.

Direct Response Marketing Rule #7: There will always be follow-up. Most buyers are not ready to buy now. It takes consistent follow-up before you can sell your products or services, in most cases. So, if your mindset is that you are going to deliver one marketing message and then quit, you won't at all be effective. When discussing the benefits of direct response marketing, I mentioned that it focuses on lead generation. The purpose of generating or capturing leads is so you can follow up consistently. You need to make up your mind that you will follow up with your leads until they buy, you reach what's your maximum allowable spend (the total amount of money that you are willing to spend to do business with a prospective buyer of your products or service before it becomes unprofitable to do business with them), or your prospects tell you that they no longer want to hear from you.

Now that we understand the benefits and ground rules of direct response marketing, we will begin the how-to journey of constructing effective marketing messages, offers and campaigns.

Coaching Assignment: Analyze your last marketing campaign to determine if it followed the rules of direct response marketing.

Visit www.theusbg.com to download a free direct response marketing checklist.

CHAPTER 5
LIGHTS, CAMERA, ACTION: WHO

"NO ONE REALLY KNEW WHAT WAS REAL OR NOT REAL HALF THE TIME."—JIM CARREY

Becoming a good direct response marketer begins with understanding the three major pillars of marketing. To do this, picture a three-legged stool. If you were to remove one of the legs or if the legs aren't equal in size, the stool won't be balanced and will be potentially dangerous for someone to sit on. So it is with marketing. There are three legs that are equal in importance. If you don't properly address any one of the three, your marketing won't be effective and may put you in danger of wasting marketing dollars and eventual business failure. Therefore, getting this right is critical for your business.

Knowing the above, I have a dirty little secret. One of the single greatest keys to becoming a good marketer is starting with the first leg of the stool, the market. To know the market, you need to truly understand the profile of exactly who you are marketing to. Knowing in great detail who your prospect is will help your target market feel like you are talking directly to them, as if you have been reading their very secret diary (more on this in the next chapter). If you get this part right, it makes creating messages and using the proper media to find them much easier. As a matter of fact, a mediocre message, as we will discuss in the next chapter, will do the trick if you have done an excellent job of understanding your prospect. Conversely, even if you have a great message, if you deliver it to the wrong person, you won't be successful. So, getting this targeting matter correct, truly understanding your audience is key.

There are three levels of understanding that you need to have about your target market if you are going to market to them effectively. The first level is the demographics. These are basic data points about your target that include the following: age, gender, income, family size, ethnicity, education, location, pet, cars, etc. If you are marketing to a business, you will want to understand firmographics. This level includes company size, revenue, industry, geography, job title of target, vendor relations (how they buy from vendors), and number of employees. Let's walk through a few of the data points, starting with age. Consider this: You are a concert promoter and you are selling tickets to a rap concert. It stands to reason that most of your target audience is going to be under 50 years old, right? And what about their income? This is a huge one. There are too many people who are marketing their products and services to people who simply can't afford them. You can't build a business that way. Here is the final aspect that we will mention: If you are a school of higher education looking to enroll people in a master's degree program, it stands to reason that you should be marketing to those who are at least in college or already have an undergraduate degree. These examples may seem obvious. Granted, the examples are a bit oversimplified, but I mention them because so many people fail in this area by simply not taking a deep dive into the question of whom they should be targeting. The reality is that this stuff isn't overly complex. It is pretty simple in concept. It just isn't easy in application, yet this is a great start.

If you are targeting business, here are a few other examples. How about the fact that you wouldn't invest most of your time selling employee development services to a business that doesn't yet have employees. Yes, you could speak to them early to plant seeds. But, spending a lot of time targeting them wouldn't be the best use of your time. Also, if you are selling a marketing product to a business, you don't want to invest your time marketing to someone who oversees customer service. There are more examples that I could share. However, I hope I have made the point that understanding general demographics is important. As an aside, allow me to say about marketing to businesses that you are NOT actually marketing to a business. You are marketing to a specific person or persons in a business. This is a critical point to keep in mind as we discuss the second and third levels of understanding that you need to have about your target.

Unfortunately, if business owners do any targeting at all, they often stop at the demographic level. As you read above, demographics are very important. However, it is ill-advised for you to stop at this level of targeting because this level is woefully incomplete for almost every single business. This is because of what you will read mentioned again and again: People buy emotionally and justify it rationally. Using only demographic information doesn't do much of anything to help understand the emotions associated with why someone will buy your product or service. You can actually have two people in the same demographic who are buying for completely different reasons. So, if your marketing is generic, based solely on demographic information, you will miss out on a great number of opportunities. Remember this: When you try to market to everyone, casting a net that most people can fit into, you end up marketing to no one at all. To move closer to where your marketing needs to be, we need to move on to level number two.

The second level of understanding that you need to have about your target market is their psychographic profile. Psychographics include personality type, religious beliefs, political views, lifestyle, attitude, and personality. If you are selling to a business, this list would include vision, mission, values and company culture. But remember that, when you are selling to a company, you are still selling to a person, so, you need to consider both the company profile and the profile of the person whom you are targeting within the company as much as possible. Let's break down a few of these as well. As you move beyond demographics to psychographic information, you get a closer understanding of what drives the emotions of a person. For example, if you are selling to someone who is adventurous, you will market to them much differently than you would to a couch potato. How about political views? More than likely, you will approach someone who is highly conservative much differently than you would someone who is an extreme liberal. Hillary Clinton supporters are going to have much different internal drivers than those who love Donald Trump. When marketing to businesses, a highly goal-oriented, for-profit culture is going to be different than a go-with-the-flow nonprofit or governmental organization. What drives them is different, so how you market to them needs to be different.

When entrepreneurs do a decent job at the demographic level of understanding their target, they often stop there. Unfortunately, many of them never move to psychographic information. But, the true holy grail of targeting which is rarely ever reached is the third level of understanding, which is what I refer to as "Soul Graphics." So many people are living quiet lives of desperation and many of them just want to feel that they are understood. Not only that, but people want to do business with people that they know, like, and trust. Understanding "Soul Graphics" will help you with just that. This level includes dreams, fears, major problems and secret desires. When you can truly speak to someone's dreams, helping them to overcome their fears and major problems, your marketing is going to be stellar. You should do your best to find out things like: What is keeping your prospects from sleeping at night? Why are they restless, staring at the ceiling? What is preventing them from truly having peace and how can you and your product or service help them with this? When you can combine all three levels of understanding into your marketing, then you will have a great handle on exactly who it is that you are targeting.

One of the best exercises that I can recommend that will help you to create a very detailed profile of your target market is based on an exercise that I completed while in a GKIC training in Florida. GKIC is one of the top direct response marketing companies in the world and its training program had us become method actors. Method acting is highly controversial in Hollywood because actors try to replicate the life circumstances, mannerisms, and emotional feelings of the character portrayed, often never breaking character during filming so that they can give a realistic, legitimate and dramatic performance. The problem with this type of acting is the fact that so many actors have a hard time coming back to reality once the film is done, so use the following method with caution. It is lights, camera, and action time. Here is the exercise: Become your ideal customer, client, or patient. Then write a letter describing who you are in great detail. Among the things that your letter will answer will include, but not be limited to are the following: Describe your background and how it has shaped you. Where do you live and why? Where do you fall in society? How is it that you have become who you are today? What are beliefs that you hold near and dear to your heart? What do you truly want in life? Why aren't you doing it right now? Are the barriers hindering you truly insurmountable? Is fear holding you back? Finish this statement, "If I could just _____." What would you be willing to do to fulfill that statement? How would life be different? Finally, how will the product or service that you offer help you to get the outcomes that you are truly looking for?

After seriously becoming your ideal customer, client, or patient, you will want to come back to reality so that we can move on to the second leg of the stool in the next chapter.

Coaching Assignment: Determine who your ideal customer, client or patient is.

Visit www.theusbg.com to download a free target audience tool.

CHAPTER 6
READING MY DIARY: WHAT

**"JUST THINK OF ME AS THE PAGES IN YOUR DIARY."—
ALICIA KEYS**

In the last chapter, you learned the three levels of understanding that you need to have about your target market. This was a prerequisite to the second leg of the stool, which is the message. Now that we know who it is that we are targeting on a deep level, we can create messages and offers that are irresistible to them. In this chapter, we will walk through the exact steps to creating messages that are truly irresistible to your target.

If you are going to create a compelling or irresistible message, there are seven things that you need to keep in mind.

#1. It is NOT about you. Too often, marketing messages and websites are created that spend too much time focused on themselves when it should be focused primarily on the needs of the target market. The reality is that your market doesn't really care about you. They care about themselves. They care about you to the extent that they believe that you are credible and competent enough to deliver what you promise to them.

#2. Be specific. Specific promises are much more effective than general promises. For example: Promising "I will help you increase revenue by 10%" is much more powerful than simply promising "I will help you increase revenue." Using specific bullet points will always outperform more generic messages.

#3. Focus on outcomes. Many of us were taught to focus on features and benefits. But this teaching was wrong. The primary focus should be on the outcome provided by the features and benefits. Remember, people are really buying for a particular outcome, even if they aren't able to pinpoint what the outcome is.

#4. Touch the emotions. This is something that I briefly mentioned in the last chapter. People buy emotionally (and justify it rationally). So, if people make emotional buying decisions, you should spend most of your time speaking to their emotions, while providing enough detail for them to rationalize the emotional decision that they made.

#5. Be bold. Because there are so many options for almost everything that people may want, you have to be bold in your marketing. Your marketing should be as bold as you can ethically, legally, and operationally make it. To be clear, I am NOT saying that you should make hollow claims just to get business. What I am saying is that if you have the goods, you want to tout how what you have is going to significantly impact the life of your target market.

#6. Give value. Too often we expect customers, clients, and patients to take the risk of doing business with us prior to us providing value to them. Give value, then expect the law of reciprocity to take over. We need to take on the risk of adding value and not getting a customer, client, or patient instead of placing our prospects at risk.

Risk reversal is one of the greatest tools in our marketing arsenal.

#7. Generate leads. The likelihood of most of our prospects buying from us immediately may not be too great. Therefore, becoming a good direct response marketer means that you should always do your best to capture the lead so that you can cultivate the relationship and follow up in the future. As mentioned earlier, only a small percentage of the population is ready to purchase anything right now, so if your marketing is one and done, you have lost before you even get started. Lead generation allows you to multiply the impact of the dollars you invested into marketing. In most cases, the amount of your revenue is in direct proportion to the size of your list of prospects that you are cultivating. So, you must always capture leads and build your list.

Creating a Compelling Message Structure
There are seven key components to creating a compelling message.

#1. AIDA - This is an acronym that you should burn into your memory. It represents the general format that all of your marketing messages should follow: Attention | Interest | Desire | Action. Whenever you do any marketing, remember that the very first thing that you have to do is to get someone's attention. We are inundated with messages every day. You have to cut through it by getting people to stop just long enough to decide if they are going to read your message. The second thing you have to do after getting someone's attention is to make sure that you get them interested in your message. It is very possible to get someone's attention quickly but lose it because they aren't interested in what you are saying. After winning their interest, you need to build a desire for the solution that your product or service offers. And this is immediately followed by a specific action. The remaining six points below go into great depth on how to effectively apply AIDA.

#2. USP - This stands for "unique selling proposition." To create a successful business that avoids price suppression and has compelling marketing, you have to be able to answer the following two questions:

(1) Why should someone do business with you instead of someone else?

(2) What is so special about what you are offering that will cause someone to do anything at all if they are not already thinking about purchasing your type of product or service?

The two questions above are adapted from the teaching of Dan Kennedy, one of the world's top direct response marketers. There are numerous ways to creating a unique selling proposition. Here are seven of the most effective ways:

(1) Repositioning - One of the best ways to describe how you can reposition your business is by using Subway as an example. Subway is a fast food alternative but they repositioned themselves in the market as a weight loss company. They did this by mimicking almost everything about how the weight loss industry markets their services. Picture Jared, their previous spokesperson, and the image of his before and after pictures. Or, picture some of the athletes that they used with the message being

communicated that Subway is what healthy, elite athletes eat.

(2) Speed - Speed is a great USP if you have a system that supports your ability to outperform your competition. A good example of this might be a car shop that changes oil in 15 minutes or less. Speed can be a great tool because people in search of speed with quality are generally less price sensitive.

(3) Niche - Using a niche group is a great way to develop a USP. One of the most common examples used by Dan Kennedy is by highlighting vitamins. If you have ever been in a vitamin store, you have probably gone down an aisle searching for a vitamin for a particular purpose, such as boosting the immune system. In doing so, you may have discovered that there were 20-30 different vitamins that claim to do the same thing. So, unless you have been given a specific recommendation, you won't have a whole lot of fun trying to choose. Now, imagine that you are an airline pilot or a recreational pilot looking for vitamins that will keep your eyes healthy. You go into the vitamin store and you see an entire aisle filled with vitamins that promise the exact same thing. The only thing that differs is the company offering it. Then, in that same aisle, you happen to run into a vitamin that is clearly labeled "for airline pilots" and this product is priced considerably higher than the other products. There is no doubt that this is the product that you will gladly purchase, even at the much greater cost. Why? Because something in your mind triggers the idea that this specific product is exactly for you, exactly what you need. Truth be told, it is pretty much the exact same formula as the rest of the vitamins. But, because this vitamin was promoted "for

airline pilots," it is the one that you are convinced is the best for you. This is the power of a niche.

(4) Price Advantage - This is simple. If, like Walmart, you match or beat the price of any of your competitors, it is an amazing way to stand head and shoulders above your competition. However, the vast majority of businesses won't be able to compete like Walmart can. So, in most cases, unless you have significantly proprietary systems and products, it is always wrong for you to build a business by trying to be the low-cost provider. Most people try to undercut the market on price because they have no other distinguishing value to offer to their market. This very section is designed to help you to eliminate this. So, if I wasn't clear already, allow me to restate that in most cases, you should NOT try to compete as the low-cost provider.

(5) Combination (Speed and Guarantee) - To illustrate the value of using multiple ways to develop a USP, I will use Domino's Pizza as an example. Actually, this example is very well-known in the world of direct response marketers and is probably my favorite. The unique selling proposition for Domino's for years was, "Fresh, Hot Pizza Delivered in 30 Minutes or Less, Guaranteed." Now, on the surface, this may not mean much to you but this USP showed an extraordinary understanding of their target market. The first Domino's restaurants were located near college campuses and college students were a primary target. Here is what makes this so special. On college campuses, you had a host of kids who smoked marijuana regularly. Well, if you are smoking marijuana, you are obviously in no condition to drive. And, one of the things that happens to you after smoking marijuana is that you get the munchies.

Also, they are in college, so they are probably broke. So, let's recap: Students are high and can't drive. They are hungry and they are broke. So, what better way to market to them than by offering some fresh, hot food and guaranteeing that it will be there within a certain amount of time or it is free. This is the best of all worlds. It is hot, reminding them of home cooking; it comes to them because they can't drive. And, there is the possibility of them getting it for free, which works because they are a broke college student. This very USP allows Domino's to build a massive business for several decades.

(6) Try Before You Buy - This is another simple one. It allows you to reverse the buyer's risk by allowing her to try something out before making a decision. This often yields positive results. An old but very cool example of this is what is known as the "puppy dog" close. This is when a pet store salesman allows parents to take a puppy home to try the puppy out before making a final decision. Of course, the children would immediately fall in love with the puppy and would in no way allow the parents to return it. This is pretty powerful stuff and we see so many offshoots of this today including auto sales. Drive it off the lot, try it. And, if you don't like it, you can bring it back within X amount of time.

(7) What Do You Hate - This works when it is obvious that your market clearly hates something. When you find real pain like this, where people really do hate something, you can create some awesome marketing messages, assuming that your product or service eliminates this issue. Think of how badly people hate losing loved ones to cancer. Imagine if you had the secret cure for all cancers? Or, on a lighter note, how about people who hate getting

into cold cars? Automatic starters and multi-car garages help to eliminate this. There are many more that I could list. But, simply ask yourself: What do you hate? In most cases, if there was a product available to solve your issue and you were able to stretch your budget to afford it, you wouldn't think twice about buying.

Before you do any marketing, you should ensure that you have a strong unique selling proposition, using one or more of the ways mentioned above so that you can maximize response rates, ultimately leading to conversions or sales.

#3. Strong Headline - A strong headline cuts through the clutter of all of the other messages that we see. It is estimated that we are exposed to over 5,000 messages each and every day. This number is an astounding 1,000% increase from 30 years ago and I can assure that this number will only increase. A strong headline or email subject line or radio or television opening is 80% of the battle of effective marketing. No matter how much effort is invested in creating the body or content of your message, it will all be for nothing if your headline or opening isn't strong enough to get the attention of your desired audience. Picture this: You are in a room with 100 other people and someone with a microphone calls your first, middle, and last names. While other people heard your name being called, you are the only one who is on highest alert. This is what a strong headline should do. It should stop you from doing whatever you are doing long enough for you to at least find out what is next. Here are a few examples of strong headlines:

"Learn to Turn Your Passion into Profit and Achieve Financial Freedom in 5 Years"

"Healthy Secrets to Safely Losing 10 Pounds in 10 Days"

"Learn to Avoid Forfeiting $1750 in Tax Returns in Less than 10 Minutes"

"How to Lovingly Housebreak Your Puppy in 3 Days or Less"

"Unusual Keys to Building Trust Immediately"

While the examples above may not be perfect, think how effective each of these would be for their specific target audiences. Openings like these are what you want to write.

#4.Outcome-Based Copy - When writing outcome-based copy, you are presenting a problem and then showing how your product or service helps with the solution. After getting someone's attention with your headline or opening, you now need to read their diary to them, in a sense. As previously stated, they should almost feel like you read their diary because you know exactly how they are feeling and what they are wrestling with. In doing so, you remind them of and amplify the issue that they have and then your job is to transition them into understanding how the solution that you are offering can help. Remember, it is NOT about you. The amount of time that you spend talking about you and your company should only be enough for them to be convinced that you can actually do what you say and that you provide a credible solution to their challenges or for their desires to be met. Here are a few examples of outcome-based copy:

"How to Have an Income Explosion by Attracting a Flood of New Customers, Clients, or Patients in 90 days or less"

"Learn the 2 Secrets that will Immediately Transform Your Business into what You Have Always Dreamed"
"How I turned $3 into $30,000 in Less than 60 Days"
The final example above is one that I did personally and I will share it with you at the close of this chapter so that you have an example that brings everything you learned into focus.

#5. Clear Call to Action - So often people get to this point in their marketing and they get it wrong for one of two reasons. The first reason is that there is no real call to action. The second reason is that the call to action is confusing. At the close of a marketing message, you first need to make sure that you don't assume that someone knows what to do next. It may seem elementary. But you can't assume. You should always be guiding your prospect to the next step and you should do it authoritatively. Don't just list a number or web address. You want to specifically tell your prospect what to do. In addition, when you tell them what to do, you don't want to give them too many options out of a desire to make things convenient. In most cases, you should only have one to two options, such as call and/or visit a website. There are other combinations that you can offer. But, remember, you should stick to no more than two. And I personally prefer just one. Examples are:
"Call 333-333-3333 Today to Register"
"Visit www.www.com Now to Purchase"

#6. Set a Limiter - If you give people all of the time in the world, they will take it. Most of us are averse to being sold. Even when we need something, can afford it, and actually want it, something within us just doesn't like to be sold. This is why you should always place a limiter in your marketing. Scarcity increases urgency and often value. The two most common limiters are Time and Quantity. Examples are:

Time - "Today Only" or "This offer Expires on..."

Quantity - "Only 100 Spots Available" or "Only 50 Toys Left"

Be mindful of the fact that, even though you will market to someone consistently, you may only have one opportunity where you have them as a captive audience, so you want to do your best to make an offer and to create urgency for them to act now. If you know that your product or service is going to put them in a better place, you have to help them to do what is in their own best interest.

#7. P.S. - This means postscript. When writing letters or emails, we have been trained that the second most important part of a message after the subject or headline is the postscript. It is the second most read part of a letter or email. The postscript tells us that there was something so important that we had to include it as the bookend to our message. This also holds true for other media like radio and television. It is the "oh, by the way" at the end of a message and it is often a good place to add a strong reason or reminder to act now or to generate a lead. Examples are:

"P.S. If you can't attend the event, be sure to visit www.www.com to download a free copy of X"

"P.S. Don't forget, the first 5 people who purchase will get a 25% discount"

If you follow the guidelines for creating irresistible messages and offers, your marketing will be much more effective. As mentioned, the messages that you create should make your audience feel like you have been reading their very secret diary. Allow me to share a personal example by referring back to one of the previous headlines, "How I turned $3 into $30,000 in Less than 60 Days." I used to sell what are called "turnkey" properties to investors around the world. A turnkey property is a property that my partner and I would buy, fully rehab, place a well-screened tenant with professional property management into, and then sell to investors for the cash flow. When I got into the business, I had no intention of scaling. This is because I knew that the retail market would eventually drive property values up, making higher prices less attractive to investors. Nonetheless, I enjoyed working with people around the world and making good money while doing so. As I ramped that business down, I still had good contractors who used to work on the houses and I wanted to keep them employed, so I decided to start a rehab management service for property managers. I have to provide some additional context so that the following marketing message makes sense. When starting my company, I sent this exact letter to my prospective clients:

DON'T LET DETROIT GENERAL CONTRACTORS DRIVE YOU NUTS!

Dear Fellow Detroit Real Estate 'Preneur,

To get your attention, I printed this on yellow paper and included some pistachio nuts. I did this because I had to discover the hard way how Bad General Contractors can Ruin your Business and Client Returns!

If you have ever experienced any of the following, then you know just how frustrating and costly it can be to work with General Contractors to get your Investment Properties in Showcase Condition:

1. Long Delays in Rehab Completion
2. Botched Rehab Jobs that Cost Double Your Budget to Fix in Time and Money
3. Contractors that Pull Disappearing Acts
4. "Break-Ins" and Missing Material
5. General Lack of Professionalism
6. City Inspection Deficiencies
7. Unhappy Clients
8. Etc...

If you can identify with any of the above and want to avoid this in the future, WE CAN HELP! If you are frustrated and need jobs turned around quickly, WE CAN HELP! We have built relationships with GREAT contractors that do excellent and timely work in the Metro Detroit Area. If you need a job done well and you need it done quickly, we can MANAGE THE PROCESS SO YOU DON'T HAVE TO. You can turn your properties over to us and we can handle everything needed to get your properties to attract the best renters and buyers. And, we do this in a timely manner with highly competitive prices...

ASK ABOUT OUR 3 WEEK JOB COMPLETION GUARANTEE
ASK ABOUT OUR UTILITY HEADACHE REMOVAL SERVICE

CALL Ian Watts TODAY and receive a FREE Hot WATER TANK with your 1st Full Rehab (Worth over $450)

Offer Expires on XXXXXX

CALL Ian Watts TODAY at XXX-XXX-XXXX

P.S. Even if you don't need any rehabs done right now, email Ian Watts TODAY at (XXXXX) and request a FREE REPORT on the GREATEST THREAT FACING DETROIT PROPERTY INVESTORS OVER THE NEXT 36 MONTHS AND WHAT TO DO ABOUT IT!

In no way was this marketing piece perfect. Perfection is something that we will discuss in a future chapter. However, it was highly effective. In fact, it was so effective that I received a 10% response rate after sending this out via direct mail to my prospects' offices. This is an astounding return when you consider the fact that getting a 1%-3% response rate is burning up the charts by traditional standards.

While I won't deconstruct the entire letter, there are few things that I will highlight to help you understand why the response rate was so high.

I had a deep understanding of my market. This understanding helped me not only craft messages that would get a response but it also informed the delivery method of my mailing. First, property management companies collect rent from tenants, who often mail it to their offices. So, I included the letter that you read above in a standard white envelope without including a return address label. The address was handwritten in red ink. I did this because handwritten letters drastically outperform non-handwritten letters. I wrote in red ink because a client, rather than a business, is more likely to write in such a color.

I included two stamps on the letter. This is because two stamps outperform one stamp. And both of these stamps were crooked and upside down. This is because crooked stamps outperform straight stamps. Remember this: Whenever you send direct mail, the first goal is to have your prospect open it.

You also read in the note that I included a bag of pistachio nuts at the top of the letter. I did this because dimensional mail, mail that is bulky, is typically placed at the top of the mail pile. And, because I targeted property management companies, they had to assume that one of their clients might have sent actual money in the mail. Not only this, but it was a cool gag because the headline was about being driven nuts. Whenever you can, use dimensional mail for direct mail. The reality is that even a strong headline won't do you any good if you can't get your message opened in the first place. And, the more human senses you can touch with your marketing, the better it will. In my case, they could see, touch, smell and even taste my message if they wanted to.

The final thing that I will say about this letter is that I actually printed my message on lined yellow paper torn from notepads just so that it stood out. If my prospects didn't respond to this letter, the very next week I sent them another letter with a headline that read, "I AM ALL TORN UP" and I included torn-up sheets of paper. I basically stated that last week I sent them a letter and they didn't respond. I then repeated the exact same thing that was in the first letter. In doing so, not only did I get a 10% response rate, but my partner and I generated $30,000 in revenue in less than 60 days. What is amazing is that, when I met each prospective property management client who responded, I spent the first 15 minutes of each new client meeting discussing who did my marketing? They actually brought my letters to the meeting and we had a time with them. At that time, I wasn't doing any small business coaching. As I consider things now, I should probably reach out again. They wanted and needed help! Ok, I digress.

If I wasn't so passionate about coaching, I may have remained in the rehab management business. But, honestly, I don't have the temperament or the desire to manage contractors. In many cases, they are a different breed. My former partner managed them while I focused on bringing in the business.

I knew that this chapter would be pretty meaty. But I hope that, after taking a deep dive into the concepts and seeing an actual example, you are now armed and dangerous enough to begin crafting irresistible offers and messages for your business. In the next chapter, we will discuss the best way to deliver your messages.

Coaching Assignment: Create your first direct response marketing message.

Visit www.theusbg.com to download free direct response marketing templates.

CHAPTER 7
MY TRIBE: WHERE

"EVERYONE IS A PART OF A TRIBE."—UNKNOWN

Now that you have learned how to effectively create a profile of your prospective customers, clients, or patients and how to write irresistible messages and offers, the final leg of the stool is the actual delivery of your message, which means media. Marketing media is simply a collection of eyeballs. You have to find the media that will best reach your most ideal prospects or "tribe." This is a good place to state that, no matter which media you choose, the fundamental principles of direct response marketing do NOT change, despite what the "gurus" tell you about things like new media and social media. The rules of the game are still the same. The only thing that changes will be the constraints of the media that you use. Let me tell you that your kids can't eat Facebook likes. While they may boost your ego, they do not directly boost revenue. Is there a correlation between likes, ad targeting and generating business? Yes, but you can't market your service with the goal of getting likes. It still has to be with the goal of getting business. If you don't have a very well-defined approach to strategically targeting those who have liked your page or posts, you won't do well. Here is what makes direct response marketing so wonderful: It is based on human psychology and the reality is that, on a fundamental level, humans don't change much. You can rest well, confident that what you are learning in this book will remain timeless. The only things that change will be the nuances of the media used. For example, you only have a certain amount of characters on Twitter. It used to be 140 characters. Now it has been doubled to 280. The core principles of marketing didn't change. You simply have 280 characters to do so.

The beautiful thing about marketing is the level of creativity and the choices that you have. Unfortunately, the latter can be a bit frustrating. This is because choosing the best media actually requires testing and patience. There is no magic bullet. Yes, you can give yourself a head start through industry research, learning what has worked best for your industry and why. But that won't necessarily help you. To stand out, you often have to bob when many others are weaving. My goal in saying this is not to get you to be a contrarian. However, I get leery about following suit when most people are doing it. There is a reason why a small percentage of the world's most successful entrepreneurs control the vast majority of its wealth. It's because they dared to think and act differently. They become comfortable being uncomfortable outliers. More on this in the final chapter.

When choosing your media, there are three major questions that you have to answer:

1. Where is the most likely place to find your prospective customers, clients or patients? Here is a general list of media from which you can choose. This list isn't exhaustive and they all have pros and cons. But this is enough to get you started. Please note that the advantages and

disadvantages listed below are very broad. And, in many cases, a medium that is a disadvantage to your competition can and most often should be used to your advantage:

Direct Mail
Advantages: Effectiveness, Creativity, Competition Level
Disadvantages: Can Lack Efficiency

Magazines
Advantages: Price Tribe Targeting
Disadvantages: Starting Costs Can Be High for Short Life Span

Radio
Advantages: Reach Per $ Spent
Disadvantages: Loose Geographic Targeting

Newspapers
Advantages: Trust, Credibility
Disadvantages: Short Life Span

Internet Pay-Per-Click
Advantages: Quick and Efficient Market Validation, Ease of Tracking
Disadvantages: Dwindling Click-Through Rates

Blogging | Vlogging
Advantages: FREE, Personal Connection and Tribe Development
Disadvantages: Lack of Speed

Billboards

Advantages: Reach per $ Spent
Disadvantages: Message Constraints

Broadcast TV
Advantages: Prestige
Disadvantages: Expense, Decreasing Viewership

Cable TV
Advantages: Prestige at a Discount, More Exact Targeting
Disadvantages: Expense, Decreasing Viewership

2. Where is the best place for you to acquire them profitably? As mentioned, the important thing to understand about choosing your media is the fact that there are no shortcuts. You have to test and you have to be patient. Testing assumes that you are marketing in a controlled environment. In short, you need to track your results. You must demand accountability for every dollar that is spent. To clarify what tracking means, here are a few minimum metrics that you should use to track each medium:

Scenario: You invest $1,000 in pay-per-click marketing in a month. You receive 10 leads and four sales at $500 per sale for total revenue of $2,000.

(1) Total amount spent on campaign during a given period of time = $1,000
(2) Total number of leads generated by the campaign = 10
(3) Cost per lead (divide total costs by number of leads) $1,000/10 = $100
(4) Number of units sold = 4

(5) Acquisition cost (divide total costs by number of units sold) $1,000/4 = $250

(6) Total return on investment (subtract total costs from total revenue. Then divide this number, which is the difference, by the total costs.) $2,000-$1,000 = $1,000. $1,000/$1,000 = 1 or a 100% return on your investment.

Let me convince you of the importance of understanding these numbers. If you are selling a product or service that yields the numbers above and you don't plan to sell anything else to your buyers, then these numbers could be concerning under the following scenario. A $500 sale costs you $250 in acquisition costs. So, if you don't have a gross margin of at least $250, you have lost money. Here is an example, using the same numbers: If I am selling a service or an item for $500 and my gross profit per unit is $150, I am losing money on every sale. Here is how it breaks down.

Item Sales Price = $500
Cost of Sales = $350 ($500 sales price - $350 cost of sales = $150 gross profit per unit)

Acquisition Cost = $250

Sales Price of $500 - Cost of Sales of $350 - Acquisition Costs of $250 = -$100

This means that, with this particular marketing medium and your current gross profit margin, you would be losing $100 on each sale, so you can see why tracking and understanding your numbers is so important. At first blush, you see that you spent $1,000 on marketing and made $2,000 in sales. This is a 100% ROI. But this may not be enough, based on what you are selling. Assuming that you can't increase your gross profit margin per unit sold, you will need to lower your cost of sales (you do this by improving the quality of your marketing and testing different marketing media), raise your prices, improve your gross profit margin, or use a combination of all three.

3. How can you integrate a multimedia strategy into your business? One is a horrible number when it comes to marketing. Specifically, using only one medium is horrible. The main reason is that you put your business at risk. Let's say you are marketing only on broadcast television. If a major war breaks out or a natural disaster occurs, most eyes will be glued to the news. Without going into much detail, you can see how this would be a problem. In addition, using a multimedia strategy can frustrate your competition. If they see your message everywhere, it definitely has some impact on their morale. Finally, not only do you want your competition to be frustrated but you also want to magnify your presence and stature in the minds of your prospects. We discussed earlier how many messages are seen on a daily basis. So, being able to use a multimedia strategy to help cut through the clutter is always a good idea to the extent that you can do it.

Now that we have covered all three legs of the three-legged stool of marketing, there is one more piece to the marketing puzzle that will grow your results exponentially and help you to generate predictable revenue, which we will cover in the next chapter.

Coaching Assignment: Decide on at least two media types you will use to reach your ideal customers, clients, or patients.

Visit www.theusbg.com to download a free media ROI comparison tool.

CHAPTER 8
TICK TOCK: TIMING AND SEQUENCE

"THERE IS A TIME FOR EVERYTHING AND A SEASON FOR EVERYTHING UNDER THE HEAVENS."—ECCLESIASTES

Have you ever heard the phrase, "Timing is everything" or "Right place, right time"? Well, in marketing, this phrase definitely holds true. The secret sauce that allows you to exponentially enhance the results that you achieve in your marketing efforts so that you can generate predictable revenue is by knowing the exact time to market to your prospects. Before you tune out and say that it is impossible to know the exact time to market to your audience, consider the following: People's mind change with time and circumstances. As a prudent marketer and business owner, you should work really hard to determine exactly when this is and offer your best stuff at that time. And, the beautiful (and not so beautiful) thing is this, privacy is dead. Because of this, you have more access to information at your fingertips, right from your cell phone, than ever before.

Consider this: You offer counseling services to troubled teens. What do you think is the ideal time to reach out to their parents? How about when they have just got in trouble with the law? Makes sense, right? Well, in most cases, if someone gets into legal trouble, this becomes public record and there are numerous prospect list brokerage companies who can pull this information for you, such as InfoUSA.com. Knowing that you have access to lists such as these should then prompt you to develop campaigns that can be sent immediately following an incident.

How about if you run a public relations company that specializes in public scandals? Well, it would make sense to have the media scoured on a regular basis to see who will be on Santa's naughty list and who should be on your prospective client list. You could target any number of people. Among those that come to mind are politicians, celebrities, major corporations, and the like. The point is that, while people who may be included in the list above might not have been interested in your services a few days, weeks, months, or even years ago, their circumstances have changed and the urgency calls for them to take some immediate actions.

Here is a final example. What if you sold beauty products to senior women? When might be one of the best times to sell your products to them? I would argue, using proven statistics, that the best time to sell to this prospect is within 30-90 days of her birthday. Why is that? Because she is thinking about the effects of aging and her beauty fading. Yes, this may be something on her mind throughout the entire year, but the birthday is a staple time for reflection for most people. And, again, the beauty for us is that birthday lists are also easy to purchase.

I hope that I have convinced you that it is not only possible but highly probable that you can market to your prospects at exactly the right time. Now, I want to address a legitimate concern. What happens if you can't buy a list or know with specificity when the best time to market to your prospect is? If this is your concern, I have a simple solution. When you can't time your marketing, you have to embrace the fact that you should always deliver your marketing messages in sequence. Delivering your marketing in sequence simply means that you do not send only one marketing message. You should always deliver your messages in a series of three messages or more. So, if you are sending direct mail, you don't just send one letter or piece in the mail, you send at least three at specific intervals. Although we haven't taken a deep dive into systems yet, I hope I have convinced you that you are in both the marketing business and the system building business. Well, when marketing, you need to be systematic. You need to know exactly when and how you will deliver your marketing messages. This includes planning how many messages will be sent, in what order, through which media, etc. Also, what is the follow-up between direct mail pieces? Will you send one piece by mail one week and follow up via email the next? These are all questions that you have to answer if your marketing is going to exceed expectations.

Remember this: Even when you have the perfect timing, you always want to market in sequence. If you can get the timing right and you have the discipline to track and market in sequence, you are well on your way to achieving amazing results and generating predictable revenue.

Coaching Assignment: Determine the three best times to reach out to your ideal customers, clients or patients.

Visit www.theusbg.com to download free resources for chapter coaching assignments.

CHAPTER 9
YOU CAN HAVE IT ALL: TIME MANAGEMENT

"SUCCESS IS THE SUM OF SMALL EFFORTS, REPEATED DAY-IN AND DAY-OUT."—ROBERT COLLIER

I have a confession to make. The title of this chapter is misleading. Contrary to popular belief, you can't have it all. As a matter of fact, to have the type of business success that you are looking to achieve, for a season you will be able to do very little else if you want a business that will eventually afford you the money and time to do the things that you want.

I didn't think that any small business guide would be complete if we didn't talk about time management. Actually, just like the title of this chapter, even time management is a fallacy. We don't actually manage time. Time keeps moving. It doesn't stop because we have goals to achieve. Rather, we manage priorities. The reality is that what brings success is doing the right small things over a long period of time. One of the main challenges that most people, not just business owners, have is the ability to guard their time ferociously. And, for many, this isn't just an issue of having a prioritized to-do list. This also means a not-to-do-list. There will always be things that compete for your time. There will always be priorities that need to be taken care of. But the key is to ensure that the priorities that will ultimately lead to you fulfilling your goals don't become a slave to a number of other things that undoubtedly will arise. If you have read Stephen Covey's *The 7 Habits of Highly Effective People*, you may recall his time management grid that stressed that we should spend most of our time completing activities in Quadrant II, which are non-urgent but important.

Every single day, you should invest at least 20% of your day doing activities that will lead to long-term results rather than managing your business by crisis. It is a pretty well-known rule that 20% of your time and effort will yield 80% of your results, as mentioned in the introduction. Yes, emergencies will come up that you will have to stop, drop, and roll for. This happens to all of us. But, if you have done the right things over a long period of time, occasional emergencies won't derail all or even most of your progress. Now, I recognize that you may be reading this and saying to yourself that this philosophy sounds good but it doesn't seem that practical. I will get more practical in just a moment. If you are wrestling with this issue and you are finding it hard to "find" time in your schedule, I challenge you to consider the following. First, I have never found any hidden or spare time in my life. I have always had to make time for those things that are most important and this process is often really difficult on the emotions when you are a highly responsible person. But, consider this: Imagine any number of tasks that you feel like you simply can't delegate to someone else and that you have no time in your schedule to add or adjust anything else. Then imagine that you are a single parent of a beautiful baby girl who you just discovered has a rare form of cancer. As you can picture, your life has just been turned upside down and your mind is racing a million miles per minute. You find out that the treatment plan is aggressive and will require 20 hours out of your week for the next year, if you are lucky, away from your business. Without question, you would do whatever you needed to do to ensure that you are there with your baby girl every step of the way. Because you are a single parent and your business pays the bills, including insurance, which you now need more than ever, shutting down shop isn't an option. Besides that, it isn't just your livelihood, but you also have employees and vendors to consider who are also counting on you, not to mention that you love your business. Burying your head in the sand isn't an option, so you make the necessary adjustments— adjustments that, prior to the news about your daughter, you couldn't even fathom. While your real-life circumstances are probably not that extreme, you need to force yourself into this type of exercise whenever you seem to get too busy to schedule and maintain at least 20% of your time working "on" your business as opposed to "in" it, as Michael Gerber from E-Myth says. Working on your business will allow you to work on the strategic initiatives that will create long-term success. Working in your business allows you to work only on the tactical level. While both are important, only one will allow you to truly build the business of your dreams, and that is investing 20% of your time in strategic, long-term goal fulfillment activities.

Everything you do has a time value attached. As a result, you need to schedule time to complete each activity that is important during the day. Even critical thinking and break times should be included in your schedule. I recommend that you not have any time period longer than 15 minutes in your day that is not accounted for. I am not saying that you should fill your schedule to the hilt with activities. This is neither wise nor healthy. But what I will say is that it is much easier to waste valuable time if you don't have your actual time accounted for, even breaks. Too often, people neglect break time and that is a mistake. Actually, it is a mistake that causes mistakes simply due to fatigue.

The most important activities, strategic activities, should be scheduled early in your day. Just like muscles, our willpower gets fatigued. So, after long days that are often mentally and emotionally draining, we set ourselves up for failure if we wait until the end of the day to do those things that are important but non-urgent. Stephen Covey explains, "The key is not to prioritize what is on your schedule, but to schedule your priorities." So that you don't run out of willpower to do those things that are of greatest priority, they should be scheduled early, while you are fresh and while the demands of your business and life for the day haven't fully engulfed you. You will almost always find that if you don't have a plan for your day, something or someone else will. No matter how badly you want to succeed, it simply won't happen until you become good at treating time as the most precious resource that it is.

As mentioned earlier, before discussing the specifics of what an ideal schedule should include, it is worth taking a deeper dive into the things that should be included on your NOT-TO-DO-LISTS. Listed below are some of the most common day-killers that you should avoid at all costs:

Day-killer #1: Checking your email first thing in the morning - I recognize that some of you have businesses that are heavily dependent upon email communication. This may even be how you are made aware of new business. However, checking your email first thing in the morning is a mistake. It often sets your mind, if not your entire day, on an unplanned course. Rather than checking your email first thing, schedule specific times throughout the day to review and respond to emails. It will give your mind greater peace and you will find this much more productive.

Day-killer #2: Getting distracted by social media. While it is tempting to casually scroll and see what your friends are up to and what is going on in the world, getting sucked into social media daily is a mistake. This is true even when you are posting and receiving likes and responses. Yes, getting likes and responses to posts feels good. However, remember that your kids can't eat Facebook likes and neither can your business grow based on likes alone. Yes, you can use very specific digital techniques to target people who like and engage on social media as mentioned. However, this isn't what I am referring to. I am referring to you wanting a mental break and being lured into all of the foolishness on social media. The flood of data is too great and, not only does it waste time, but it also affects your mental state. As with email, set specific times that you will allow yourself to be on social media.

Day-killer #3: Taking unscheduled calls or meetings. Not only is it okay, it is absolutely necessary to ignore unscheduled calls and to NOT take unscheduled meetings. It is really tempting to be accommodating to people who want to speak or for people who want to come in for a "quick, got-a-minute" meeting. While I can appreciate employers who believe in an open door policy, I find that it can be woefully unproductive if not monitored closely. Yes, you can have an open door policy and you can even take unscheduled meetings. But, you have to have time blocks in your schedule to do so. The same thing goes for unscheduled calls. The calls that you receive and the "got-a-minute" meetings can often wait until a daily huddle or your weekly staff meeting time. Now, I am assuming that you have a daily huddle and weekly staff meeting time with your team. If you don't, implement this right away so that you can provide the support and direction necessary for your key team members. And do this so that your team members can see you model key priority and time effectiveness principles.

Day-killer #4: Allowing the emergencies of others to offset your day. In no way do I want you to think that I am a mean ogre. Telling you to do your best to ignore the emergencies of others may make me sound like that. But, consider this: If you spend a significant amount of your time putting fires out for others, you can rob them of the learning experience of being able to work through things themselves. Also, you often find that what others consider to be an emergency often is not as big as it seems; it's only big in their minds because they are so close to it. Finally, dealing with the emergencies of others is a great way to derail your day. I suggest setting up a simple ranking system for "emergencies." You can do this from Level 1 to Level 5. And how you categorize each level will determine your level of response, if any response at all.

Day-killer #5: Making commitments before analyzing the effect on your schedule. As business owners and leaders, we have to make a myriad of decisions each and every day. Most of these decisions are made with imperfect information, thanks to the life that we have chosen as entrepreneurs. When it isn't a key decision that bets the farm, it is often best to review data that you have and quickly make up your mind. However, when the time required is significant, you shouldn't make a decision before its impact has been thoroughly analyzed.

Day-killer #6: Operating without a clear, scheduled plan for the day. As we talk about time (priority) management and protecting your daily schedule, this actually assumes that you have one. At no point should you enter any day without intentionality, your top three to five goals, and a scheduled agenda. If you don't operate that way, you are severely limiting your effectiveness. So, allow me to simply say: STOP IT!

Day-killer #7: Fill in the blank. While all of the aforementioned day-killers are common, you may find that there is something else that steals your day. If so, you need to acknowledge what it is and determine what you will do to eliminate it. You should strive to win every single one of your days. This is done by strategically planning and scheduling every single day and by guarding it ferociously.

Before we wrap up this section, I want to provide a list of things that a successful day often includes. You should consider the list to follow and begin planning your days accordingly:

❏ Spiritual development time
❏ Personal development time
❏ Exercise time
❏ Meal times

❏ Personal grooming time
❏ Commute time
❏ Top three to five goal completion times
❏ General work time
❏ Meeting prep time
❏ Got-a-minute times
❏ Break times
❏ Family and friend time
❏ Reflection & next day preparation time
❏ Sleep time

While you may find that there are some other critical activities that you need to include in your schedule, the list provided is a pretty good start. Effectively scheduling and managing priorities is critical to your success. Not doing so is detrimental not only to your business but to your personal life as well. Ben Franklin is quoted as saying, "You may delay but time will not." We are all given the same amount of time each day, be sure to invest it wisely.

Coaching Assignment: Complete an ideal schedule.
Visit www.theusbg.com to download a free ideal schedule tool.

CHAPTER 10
FREE AT LAST: DEVELOPING EFFECTIVE SYSTEMS

"TIME IS BORROWED AND WE DON'T KNOW WHEN OUR
DEBT WILL BE CALLED DUE."—UNKNOWN

Ask yourself: If time and money weren't a challenge, what would you be doing? Building a successful business allows you to answer this question. Success in any business is achieved when the business does what you have designed it to do. Obviously, success is relative, based on your individual goals. So, for the purpose of providing better context for this chapter, allow me to impose two tangible benchmarks of success. I recognize that many people reading this have goals that extend well beyond what I am about to share. But, because I work with many budding entrepreneurs, please indulge me. Success is when you have created a business that generates the monthly post-tax cash flow that you desire and that gives you the freedom of time to live the life of your dreams and achieve your WHY. Again, I recognize that my definition may not include all that you may have imagined success being for your business, but I am convinced that this is a good starting point. And this chapter will help you get there. During the first portion of this book, we learned how to generate predictable revenue and the cash flow that we want by becoming direct response marketers. But generating predictable revenue and cash flow alone does not allow freedom. That is only half of the equation. What will allow you to build a business that will grow and give you freedom of time is learning how to develop effective systems.

I think that people too often complicate things unnecessarily. This is especially so when discussing business systems, so it is my deepest hope that I can demystify it for you. To begin, let's discuss what a system is. As defined by Merriam Webster's Dictionary, "A system is a set of principles or procedures according to which everything is done." In my own words, a system is a set of written, step-by-step instructions for every key area of your business. In short, it is a written how-to guide for your business. Here is what you want to consider: What would happen if you didn't work in your business for six months? Unfortunately, for too many business owners, this would mean that their business would completely collapse. Now, in fairness, I recognize that most early-stage small businesses wouldn't be able to survive this. This is because the business is driven by the passion of the entrepreneur. And rightfully so. Not only that, but in early-stage companies, revenue hasn't reached a point where the proper staffing levels are in place. Now that this caveat is out of the way, I can address the core challenge.

Most established businesses with sufficient revenue and staffing will fail or, at best, will cease growing if the owner leaves for six months. That happens because most business owners are building companies that are too dependent upon them and other key leaders in their business. I do understand that leadership is important but building a business that is too heavily dependent on the talent and intellectual capital of you or other key leaders is a mistake. This mistake will either stifle growth and/or make the owner a slave to the business. On the contrary, business owners should strive to build a systems-dependent business with people in place to oversee these systems.

If you build a systems-dependent business, you won't have to hire the most expensive talent that you can find. Actually, when you have effective enough systems, you can hire the minimal level of talent required. This is because your business won't be reliant upon them; it will be reliant upon systems that they will oversee and improve upon. In addition, when you have a systems-dependent business, you, the owner, don't have to spend every waking hour at your place of business for it to flourish. A great way to think about systems is by picturing a toy purchased from a toy store. This toy has to be assembled before it works properly. So, when you get home, you take all of the pieces out of the box and first make sure that they are all there. After you have determined that you have all of the pieces, you take another look to make sure that you have all of the tools required to assemble the pieces. Finally, you begin the process of assembling the toy by following the step-by-step instructions. If you are anything like me, you are not mechanically inclined. To assemble the toy, I need the instructions to be written and diagrammed as if I am a two-year-old. And, if this is done, I have a toy that is fully assembled and that can be enjoyed by my kids without my further involvement. So it is with your business. To develop effective systems, there are only three things that you need to create:

1. The proper tools and access needed to help follow clearly written instructions
2. A clear, written set of properly timed, chronological instructions for all of the key areas of your business
3. People in place with the specific goal to oversee and enhance the chronological instructions for greater effectiveness and efficiency

If you have these three basic components, you will have a business that works just like the well-assembled toy and it will be positioned to grow without being dependent upon you.

Let's quickly analyze the five key areas of any business. Allow me to preface this by saying I recognize that each business has its own nuances and the intricacy levels of businesses will vary, but my goal is to help simplify this process as much as possible so that you can implement it. To do so, I have listed the five broad categories that your business must create systems for.

1. Marketing: Positioning your business and your product or service to generate leads and create sales opportunities
2. Sales: Converting sales opportunities and leads into actual sales

3. Finance: Collecting the revenue from sales, paying bills, creating and managing budgets
4. Operations: Delivering the promised product or service sold and managing the post-sale-customer experience (in partnership with marketing)
5. Leadership: Recruiting, training, inspiring and developing people

Each of the categories listed above will definitely have sub-categories and each sub-category will require systems as well. Not only this, but you may think that the definitions above are a bit incomplete. That doesn't bother me as long as the essence remains the same. I don't want you to get bogged down in your thinking. What I do want you to do is get the concept so that this is actionable for you. As a matter of fact, just know that you should start your systems development process and it will become more granular the longer you wrestle with it.

To make systems development a bit clearer, let's pretend that you own a residential cleaning business. Assume that you have followed the proper systems to generate a lead and close a sale. We will analyze a sample system as the client is transitioned from sales to operations for the cleaning service to be fulfilled. Now, stick with me here. I know that businesses will have various models for closing sales and servicing clients and I don't run a cleaning business; I am just making this up, so let's just pretend a bit for illustrative purposes.

Remember that there are three areas that you need to address to create an effective system. I have provided one-word abbreviations for them below:

System Need #1: Tools
- ☐ A telephone system to confirm the details of each client's cleaning service
- ☐ A scheduling system to schedule the cleaning between the client and the cleaner
- ☐ A customer relationship management (CRM) system to track details of each client and communicate
- ☐ Transportation for the cleaner
- ☐ GPS for the cleaner
- ☐ Uniform for the cleaner
- ☐ Specific cleaning supplies for the cleaner
- ☐ Post-cleaning gift for the client
- ☐ Post-cleaning inspection checklist
- ☐ Camera

System Need #2: Instructions
1. Sales rep transfers the call to the operations rep.
2. Operations rep conducts call with client to confirm details of cleaning, take payment method, and dispatch cleaner.
3. Cleaner drives to client home and parks at instructed location.
4. Cleaner exits car and removes all cleaning items needed for job.
5. Cleaner rings doorbell.
6. Cleaner addresses client with specific greeting upon door being opened and entering home.

7. Cleaner immediately places booties over feet upon entering home.
8. Cleaner reconfirms requested cleaning items and confirms usage of specific products.
9. Cleaner begins cleaning home in very specific order.
10. Cleaner conducts a post-cleaning inspection, pictures, and non-invasive additional business checklist.
11. Cleaner informs client of completion status, conducts post-cleaning sales summary, and present client with specialized discount for acting quickly on additional uncovered needs by cleaner.
12. Cleaner leaves special gift for client.
13. Cleaner exits home and returns to car.
14. Cleaner takes five minutes to update CRM while in car before leaving.
15. Cleaner travels to next designated place.
16. Operations Rep conducts post-cleaning survey and updates CRM.
17. Operations Rep informs sales rep of additional business opportunities if cleaner couldn't close.
18. Sales Rep contacts client to upsell services.
19. Sales Rep updates CRM.
20. Sales Rep selects and schedules automated series of messages to client.

System Need #3: People
❏ Sales Rep - Transitions the client to the operations department to schedule the cleaning.

- ☐ Operations Rep - Confirm details of cleaning, collects payment, dispatches the cleaner, and conducts post-cleaning survey.
- ☐ Cleaner - Clean house, searches for additional service opportunities.

As you can see from this example, nothing that I have listed is overly complicated. Actually, you can even see where there are holes and inefficiencies in the system above. If you noted things that are missing, such as timing or that are redundant, that is good, because it means you are actively engaged in wrestling with this system. And I have never run a cleaning business, so what I have listed may be way off. But I wanted to use an example that I thought would be easy for most people to envision and follow, even without experience in this type of business.

By going through an exercise like the one above for all of the key areas of your business, you will eventually build a business that is highly scalable and this scalability will not only give you the cash flow that you desire but the freedom of your time, not having to actually work in your business. Your business will be able to function like a well-oiled machine or that properly working toy that brings so much joy to kids if the instructions are followed during assembly.

Coaching Assignment: Create a one-page system for the five key areas of your business.

Visit www.theusbg.com to download a free systems development tool.

CHAPTER 11
DON'T BET THE FARM: LEAN METHODOLOGY

"I HATE ENTREPRENEURS WITH BEAUTIFUL BUSINESS PLANS."—BARBARA CORCORAN

Business plans suck. Yup, I said it and I won't take it back. Now that I have made such a bold statement, let me tell you what I can appreciate about business plans. First, the value in developing a good business plan is not in the actual completed plan itself; it is in the process of working through it. There is value in thinking through all of the most critical areas in business plans. Also, business plans are impressive and may even be a necessity if you are raising money from banks and investors. However, relying upon traditional business plans can really hurt you if you are dependent upon your plan to help you launch a new business, product or service.

In his *New York Times* bestselling book, *The Lean Startup*, entrepreneur and thought leader, Eric Ries, popularizes methodology that is counter to traditional business thinking. This thinking is the predominant method of both high-flying startups and major companies like Apple and Zappos. Too often startups and existing businesses alike bet the farm on a new idea using the unpredictable and dangerous, yet common approach of generating an idea, writing a business plan, raising money, and launching. The method is often to their detriment. Eric Ries defines entrepreneurship as, "A human institution designed to create a new product or service under conditions of extreme uncertainty." Business plans, especially for startups, are often based upon untested but critical business assumptions. And the business plan includes revenue projections based on these untested assumptions. You can see why this is so dangerous. In response to this dilemma, lean startup methodology should be applied.

In Chapter 1, I mentioned that I got started in the real estate business through a Carleton Sheets home study course. The single greatest thing that his home study course helped me to do was to think differently about how to approach investing with little resources and within a short period of time. So it is with lean startup methodology. At its core, lean startup methodology is designed to help you quickly and inexpensively launch new businesses, new products, or new services by removing the uncertainty of how the market will respond. The hallmark of being able to do this is by creating what is known as a minimum viable product (MVP). An MVP is a scaled-down version of your product or service so that you can answer the two most important questions that every business hinges upon, (1) Does the market want what I have to offer? (2) Can I deliver it to the market in a way that I can scale my business? Now, I know what you might be thinking. A traditional business plan accounts for these two questions because it often includes survey results. While it is a novel idea that surveys are sufficient to build a business around, they are not. Good surveys do have their place. However, they shouldn't be the sole data used to base a business upon. Here is why: When trying to determine what the market wants, a survey only informs you of what the market says that they will do. But we know that what people say they will do and what they actually do are often totally different things. On the other hand, an experiment shows you exactly what someone actually does. So the goal becomes creating quick and inexpensive experiments to learn what the market actually does, such as buying your product or taking whatever action you want them to take.

The problem that many people have with this type of methodology is that it simply makes them uncomfortable. There are several reasons. The first reason is that it is simply safer and more exciting to dream about what you expect than to actually test it. But, if you have mastered your emotions and the former isn't your challenge, you may still struggle with having to scale down your vision or release things before they have reached the level of excellence that you are accustomed to. Let's go deeper. An MVP is a scaled-down or slightly off version of what you ultimately want to build and it is produced and introduced to the market too quickly for comfort and at only a fraction of the capital that you want to invest into it. While that may be exciting for some, this makes most people uncomfortable. So that we can discuss specific examples, let's dive into three easy ways to develop an MVP:

1. Pre-sales
2. Strategic partnerships
3. Low-feature launch

Let's take a look at all three. Pre-sales is exactly what it sounds like. You sell your product or service in advance of actually having produced what you are offering. A great example of this is Zappos. Zappos is an online shoe and clothing company that produces over $2 billion in annual revenue. Its rise was meteoric and it had humble beginnings, being founded in 1999 using lean startup methodology. The major thing that Zappos had to test was whether they could build their business around a market that was ready to buy clothes, beginning with shoes, strictly online. To test this, Nick Swinmurn, the founder of Zappos, designed a quick and inexpensive experiment. He built a cheap website. He went to local retailers, got permission to take pictures of their shoes, and then added these pictures to his website. After doing this, he ran some inexpensive ads to his website to see if he could get anyone interested in purchasing. And, to his excitement, he did. Now, remember, he didn't have any actual inventory. He only had pictures on his site. So, after receiving the orders, he went back to the local retailers, purchased the merchandise at full price and shipped it himself. Notice that he didn't build a traditional business plan. He didn't go out and spend tens of thousands of dollars on a sophisticated website. He didn't go out and purchase a warehouse and fill it full of inventory. He inverted the process to discover if the market wanted what he offered and if he could provide it to the market in a way that made sense. So he pre-sold inventory, which funded his ability to purchase the inventory in the first place, while proving the viability of his offering and business model.

Strategic partnerships are another great way to build an MVP. Suppose you want to open a trucking company. And let's also suppose that you don't have the proper licensing, nor do you have a truck. With lean startup methodology, you don't let this to stop you at all. You simply find someone who already has the licensing and a truck and partner with them. You will generate the business and they will drive the truck and deliver the actual service. Remember, you are in the marketing business. So, if you discover how to drive business through the door based on your unique offering to the market, you can then look to get licensed, finance trucks, and so forth. But how bad would it suck for you to build a plan, raise funding, get licensed, buy a truck, and get stuck with this overhead, only to find out that you have built a bridge to a place that no one wants to go to? You can see how this process can help you avoid getting stuck and quickly put you in business with a website, a few legal documents, and some marketing.

A low feature launch is the third great way to ensure that your product or service is irresistible to your market. Multi-billion dollar companies use it all the time. This is especially the case with technology companies but the principles apply to any business. In general, if you want to offer a product or service that will have 20 bells and whistles, you need to reduce the number of features down to a bare minimum, the core features to ensure that what you are offering is something that the market wants. Again, it would really suck if you put all of your time and effort into making your product or service perfect, only to discover that no one wants it. A pretty notable example of this is how Apple launches their new phones with glitches and lacking certain features. Now, I am not an Apple guy, but my wife and many of my friends are Apple enthusiasts. One year, Apple launched one of their phones without a feature as simple as cut and paste. Now, they eventually fixed this. But, many other businesses wouldn't even consider such a thing. Not so with Apple. Even as I am writing, the new iPhone has some glitch that causes crazy typos. Yes, there is a fix for this as well. But, my point is, they didn't wait until their product was glitch-free and had all of its features intact. Even though they have a strong following, launching in this manner keeps them from over-building a product, just in case the market falls out of love with them.

There are many more examples that I could cite or even make up. I often make up MVPs on the spot for attendees when I am doing live trainings. If you need to build a business plan, if you are going to hit the go button on a new business, product, or service, do so after employing lean startup methodology and by building an MVP. Doing so will ensure that your business, product, or service is irresistible to your market. You want to quickly and inexpensively remove as much uncertainty associated with your business to avoid wasting your time and capital or, even worse, some investors or lenders.

Coaching Assignment: Brainstorm and create an MVP for your next product or service launch or relaunch (if you are within 90 days of a new launch).

Visit www.theusbg.com to download free resources for chapter coaching assignments.

CHAPTER 12
SUCCESS LEAVES CLUES: FOLLOWING GIANTS

"LONG AGO, I REALIZED THAT SUCCESS LEAVES CLUES, AND THAT PEOPLE WHO PRODUCE OUTSTANDING RESULTS DO SPECIFIC THINGS TO CREATE THOSE RESULTS."—TONY ROBBINS

While there are certain things that I have strongly cautioned against, there are some timeless truths I do recommend that you follow. Success does, in fact, leave clues and, if you want to generate predictable revenue and systems so that you can fulfill your small business dream, you would do well to seriously consider and employ the seven secrets of the world's most successful entrepreneurs:

Secret #1: Take Action - Nothing just happens. From the mere fact that you are reading this book, I have to assume that there are some changes that you want to make in your business and life. The reality is that change is always difficult. And, as you look to make changes, your emotions and brain will go into protection mode and do everything that it can to "protect" you from doing things that place you at "risk." But, when the temptation arises for you to turn back, resist it. Resist it violently by taking massive action. As business owners, we have to make the adjustments we know that we need to make despite how we feel. We need to do it and wait for our emotions to catch up. Emotions make great slaves but poor masters, so do it despite how you feel. I know that many actions will be tough to take because we live in a world where we constantly have to make decisions based on imperfect information. But do it anyway. Your dreams, the reasons why you are reading this book, and your ultimate WHY depend upon it.

Secret #2: Be a Continuous Learner - I heard a quote that says, "When you are green, you are growing. But, when you ripen, you begin to rot." The reality is that we will never "arrive." There is always more to learn so that we can grow. Remember that leaders are readers. There is a note that I want to add about this. Being a continuous learner does not mean that you continue to get ready to get ready to get ready. You need to deputize yourself to use what you learn to make the changes that will result in transformation as you move forward. So, while you learn continuously, be sure that you don't forget Secret #1—to take action. Certain learning will only take place in the lab of business and life as you move forward. So don't develop analysis paralysis.

Secret #3: Burn Your Boat - I have heard the story of a military leader who had a mission-critical battle that had to be won on an island that enemy fighters controlled. This leader sailed with his soldiers to the island to fight. Upon arrival, the military leader burned their boats. This is astounding to me. What was the message that he was sending to his troops? It was, "We either win or die."

There were no other options. In business and in life, we sometimes give ourselves a way of escape when things get difficult. But note that people are always watching. Employees, vendors, customers, clients or patients, competitors, and even family members. No one likes a dabbler or someone who will retreat when trouble comes. So, make up your mind that you are going to leave yourself no option but to succeed, even if you have setbacks along the way.

Secret #4: Accept Personal Responsibility - When the bottom fell out of my business in 2006, I had well-meaning friends and family who consoled me by saying that the market was the reason for my business failing and I was in good company, since businesses like GM were filing for bankruptcy. To be honest, I tried to tell myself that, too, because the pain was so great. But the reality is that the market wasn't the reason for my business failure. I was the reason. As a matter of fact, some of the greatest transfers of wealth happen during "bad" economic times. This is because you can get so much at bargain basement prices. The reality is that businesses don't actually fail. Businesses are created and run by people and our job as entrepreneurs is to steer our businesses toward profitability no matter what market we are in. So, you have to embrace the concept of extreme ownership of the results of your business and your life.

Secret #5: Get Accountability - No man is an island. We all work best in a community, even loaners. If you want to see the results that you are looking for, one of the single greatest keys is to give someone permission to hold you accountable for your goals. Accountability is so important and the results are so astounding that I don't accept clients unless they commit to getting a serious accountability partner.

Secret #6: Join a Mastermind Group - Most breakthroughs in any industry come from outside that industry. You can see this when you consider the history of drive-through window services. Akin to the accountability that a mastermind group provides, you will also benefit from the ideas, energy, the challenges and triumphs of other business owners. This is because you will be able to identify with the unique challenges associated with operating a business, glean wisdom and share best practices, even outside of your industry.

Secret #7: Get A Business Coach - "Everyone needs a coach." The previous quote is from the wealthiest person in the world (or at least he is during the time of this writing), Bill Gates. If Bill Gates, Warren Buffett, Michael Jordan, and many other icons that I could name have coaches, how much more do we need one? A coach's job is to push you more than you want to be pushed, to help you avoid danger and overcome your blind spots, shorten your learning curve, and ensure that you reach your goals. It may not feel good but it will be for your good. My greatest leaps and bounds didn't take place until I hired a business coach. All of the secrets that we covered prior to this are things that a good coach will help you with. The reason why I love running a small business coaching company is because I know how transformative coaching is for those who are serious about it.

If you take the secrets revealed in this chapter seriously, your ability to implement the changes necessary for you to generate predictable revenue and develop effective systems for growth will be a reality. And, not only this, you will have built a business that gives you the passive income and the freedom of time to achieve your WHY!

Coaching Assignment: Hire a Small Business Coach.

Visit www.theusbg.com to complete the Coaching Readiness Survey.

Resource Section

B ecause this book was created to be a guidebook, I thought it only appropriate to provide a list of resources that will be helpful for further learning and massive action. Below is a list of books that will allow you to dive deeper into the major subjects covered in each chapter.

Book References:
Chapter 1: How to Overcome Major Business and Life Obstacles
- *Start with Why* by Simon Sinek
- *Grit* by Angela Duckworth
- *Man's Search for Meaning* by Viktor Frankl
- *David and Goliath* by Malcolm Gladwell

Chapter 3: Branding
- *Book the Business* by Adam Witty and Dan Kennedy
- *Crush It* by Gary Vaynerchuk

Chapters 3-8: Direct Response Marketing
- *NO B.S. Direct Marketing* by Dan Kennedy
- *The Adweek Copywriting Handbook* by Joseph Sugarman
- *The Ultimate Sales Letter* by Dan Kennedy

Chapter 9: Priority Management
- *The One Thing* by Gary Keller and Jay Papasan
- *What the Most Successful People Do Before Breakfast* by Laura Vanderkam
- *7 Habits of Highly Productive* People by Stephen Covey
- *The Game: Win Your Life in 90 Days* by Sarano Kelly

Chapter 10: Developing Systems
- *The E-Myth Revisited* by Michael Gerber
- *Built to Sell* by John Warrillow

Chapter 11: Low-Risk Product and Service Launches
- *The Lean Startup* by Eric Ries
- *The Power of Broke* by Daymond John and Daniel Paisner

Chapter 12: Following the Path of Success
- *Think and Grow Rich* by Napoleon Hill
- *From Good to Great* by Jim Collins

Financial Freedom
- *Rich Dad Poor Dad* by Robert Kiyosaki and Sharon Lechter
- *Unshakeable* by Tony Robbins

Leadership
- *21 Irrefutable Rules of Leadership* by John Maxwell
- *Extreme Ownership* by Jocko Willink and Leif Babin
- *How to Win Friends and Influence People* by Dale Carnegie
- *Everyone Communicates, Few Connect* by John Maxwell

TAKE THE NEXT STEP

NOW THAT YOU HAVE READ THIS BOOK, IT IS TIME TO TAKE MASSIVE ACTION SO THAT YOU CAN APPLY WHAT YOU'VE LEARNED AND EXPERIENCE THE RESULTS THAT YOU DESIRE.

IAN OFFERS A RANGE OF COACHING AND TRAINING SERVICES TO ASSIST YOU IN YOUR JOURNEY.

TRAINING PRODUCTS:
FOR GROWING BUSINESSES – THE PREDICTABLE REVENUE BOOT CAMP

COACHING PROGRAMS:
MAAS (MASSIVE ACTION & ACHIEVEMENT SYSTEM)
ONE-ON-ONE MONTHLY COACHING
WEEKLY MASTERMIND GROUPS
SPECIAL COACHING AND CONSULTING PROJECTS

LIVE TRAINING EVENTS:
SEE WWW.THEUSBG.COM FOR NATIONWIDE TOUR DATES

TO LEARN MORE ABOUT HOW IAN CAN BEST HELP YOU, VISIT WWW.THEUSBG.COM TO SCHEDULE A FREE BUSINESS BREAKTHROUGH SESSION

ABOUT THE AUTHOR

 **Ian M. Watts,** the founder of SB Dream Coach, is an entrepreneur and small business coach who achieved his dream of becoming a millionaire by the age of 26. He has raised millions in capital, launched multiple businesses, and helped countless business owners to transform their thinking and businesses. He has provided coaching and training for business owners in over 40 states in the US and in many countries around the world, including China, Hong Kong, Canada, The United Kingdom, Saudi Arabia and Australia. He is a "Small Business Junkie" who created SB Dream Coach so that he could, "**...be what he didn't see**" as a young business owner.